Ordinary Life...

Touched by an Extraordinary God

May you sense the presence of the Lord in the "coincidences" in your own life

by Arlene M. Gray

Arlene M. Gray

An Ordinary Life...

Touched by an Extraordinary God

Reflections to Encourage Your Spirit
While Tickling Your Funnybone
And Touching Your Heartstrings

by Arlene M. Gray

An Ordinary Life . . .
Touched by an Extraordinary God

Copyright ©1997 Arlene M. Gray
Second Printing 1999

Cover photograph by William J. Gray
Photograph on back cover by Scott M. Gray

Scripture verses are from the Holy Bible, King James Version

All rights reserved. No part of this publication may be reproduced, stored in a retrieval system, or transmitted in any form or by any means, electronic, mechanical, photocopying, recording, or otherwise, except for the inclusion of brief quotations in a review or article, without prior written permission.

Published by
Turnage Publishing Co., Inc.
6737 Low Gap Road
Blairsville, GA 30512
sturnage@peachnet.campus.mci.net

ISBN 1-880726-12-2

Printed in the USA by

MORRIS PUBLISHING

3212 East Highway 30 • Kearney, NE 68847 • 1-800-650-7888

Acknowledgments

It is with special appreciation that I acknowledge my gratitude to the many friends and relatives without whose help and encouragement this book would never have come to fruition. In alphabetical order only, and not because of importance, I'd like to specifically recognize the input of Arlene (not me/another one), Billy, Christy, Frank, Genevieve, Lucy, "K-k-k-katie," Margaret, Marlene, Mary, Pam, Patty, Paul, Rachel, Ruth, Scott, Sharon, Stephanie, Tammy, Terri, Tommy, and William. To those with the ministry of encouragement, the ministry of discernment, or the ministry of laughter---and you each know which category you fall into---a million thanks; my heart is full to overflowing with gratitude and sweet remembrances, and many of you will find the story of how you impacted my life within the pages of this book.

To a dedicated editor who, although we had never met, agreed to lend assistance and help where needed, I owe a debt of thanks. (Note: A mutual friend put me in touch with a man who had pastored a church for 25 years, taught in colleges, edited an international Christian magazine for thirteen years, authored books of his own and now holds revivals wherever called.) *I still cannot believe that a man of his caliber and experience agreed to edit my first work.* Rev. William E. McCumber . . . a gazillion thanks! I had to put just one more exclamation point here, even though you made me take out hundreds of them throughout the manuscript. Thank you for stepping out in faith and for your wonderful words of encouragement.

To my husband Bill, who patiently stepped in to run the farm single-handedly and often endured dinner of a sandwich and chips while I labored uninterruptedly at the computer, and who was willing to wait for "just the right light" to take the photograph that eventually became the cover of this book, my deepest appreciation. Thank you for believing in this project. You've not only earned a filet mignon supper, but I promise you one to celebrate the publication of this "never-ending book."

But mostly, it is with deepest appreciation that I stand in awe before my Lord and Savior, the Creator of the Universe, Who set this task before me and then enabled me to do what I had never done before. His Word (1 Thessalonians 5:16-18) tells me to "Be joyful always; pray continually; give thanks in all circumstances for this is God's will for you," and when I am obedient to that command He is faithful to shed His grace and His power on me. What an awesome and extraordinary God!

Dedication

This book is lovingly dedicated--with hugs and kisses--to two precious, sweet, affectionate, wonderful children, Stephanie and Brandon. (I'm their gran'ma; I can be partial!)

TABLE OF CONTENTS

PREFACE/The "How-cum" of this Book

It's funny how something as seemingly insignificant as a pesky cough can be the catalyst for change in one's life. For me, I had an annoying ongoing cough for *months* that didn't seem to respond to any treatment whatsoever. For the most part, I just "lived with it," but when a doctor said (in a rather relaxed tone of voice), "Well, maybe we ought to do a laryngoscopy and if there is malignancy we might have to remove your voice box," that really got my attention. I started thinking of all the things I'd want to say before I lost the ability to speak, and mostly I wanted to be able to tell my precious grandchildren about their grandmother and how the Lord had walked with her throughout her life.

I went to another doctor who thought a long-lasting cough might indicate the possibility of cancer, and ordered a mammogram. When the results came back with a "shadow," I was sent back for more pictures. I remember saying to the technician, after the third x-ray, that things weren't looking good. It made me reflect on the fact that our life here is very temporary, and if there was anything I wanted to leave behind for my grandchildren, I ought to get busy and see to it. Since they were still pre-schoolers, I started thinking that maybe I should write down some of the incidents in my life in which the Lord's hand was evident, so they could read about them when they got older.

At the same time that I was dealing with the cough, my old foe, depression, raised its ugly head once again. I went to a Christian counselor for two visits and he gave me a homework assignment: I was to write a letter to myself that I believed the Lord would write to me. For about ten days, I didn't work on the assignment, but then one morning I *leaped* out of bed (not my usual manner of waking up in the morning), and couldn't wait for the computer to boot-up so I could place my itchy fingers on the keyboard. In a few minutes a three-page message had emerged---the power and thrust of which was incomprehensible! It took my breath away! I knew it was an inspired message and that the author was my loving Father, Lord and Savior. I tried to read it to my Bible study group the next day, but it was so powerful I was unable to get past my tears. The letter became renewed impetus for writing down all the stories I could remember.

When the medical results came back favorable, I realized I had been given an opportunity to glimpse into the im-permanency of life and to leave a meaningful legacy behind. I thought there might be six to eight little stories. However, as I started writing, I was struck by new awarenesses that I hadn't fully understood previously, and before I knew it there were over two dozen incidents that flooded my memories. The next thing I knew, my desire to share my life with my grandchildren grew into this little book with over sixty recollections. From the comments of people who read the first edition of the book, I've seen evidence that the Lord has used it to minister to people to bring them hope and reassurance.

This collection of stories is evidence that the Lord works through very ordinary people to accomplish His extraordinary deeds, and that all He seeks is an open heart and an obedient spirit. I can hardly believe all the memories that have surfaced since I began my journalistic journey, and my prayer over each copy is that you, the reader, will receive encouragement and strength for your own journey. One of my favorite songs expresses my thoughts best, "Our God is an awesome God. . .He reigns over heaven above". . .and over our lives as well! My life has been blessed by knowing the Creator of the universe, who knows me by name! And He knows *you*, too! He has spoken through the ages and continues to speak today, if only we open our ears to hear. May these stories bring you to a new awareness of how events that seem like "coincidences" are actually the *visible* hand of God reaching into our lives, if we just open our eyes to see and our ears to hear!

One day our life on earth will end, and if mine were to end today I would have known the joy of walking with the Lord through mountaintop experiences and the comfort of His presence through the deepest valleys; and that same assurance can be yours. He longs for fellowship with us; in fact His purpose in creating us was for fellowship with Him! He stands outside our heart and knocks, and those who open the door for Him to enter are blessed with unfathomable joy. If you feel the tap-tap-tapping on your heart, open the door (the handle is on the *inside!*) and let the King of the universe enter and wrap His loving arms around you. He is Father, Brother, Husband, Friend, Comforter, Counselor, Savior, Healer of the broken-hearted. And He loves you with an everlasting and never-ending love!

My prayer is that the Lord will use these stories to help you discover that your *own* life is filled with miraculous, wondrous, indescribable events in which, upon reflection, you can directly trace the hand of God!

Dear Lord,
     You know everything about me, and I know You are aware that I am once again battling my enemy of depression, and You know the cause. My counselor gave me the assignment of writing a letter that I believe You would write to me in these circumstances. And so, Lord, I ask You to speak.

Dear Arlene, my precious child,

     I am pleased that you have sought this letter from me. In fact, whenever you seek Me, it delights Me! In instances like that, it opens the door for Me to shower you with My grace and My love.

     You have been feeling somewhat "down," lately. I know this, and I've watched you battle with depression from time to time over the years. I remember how debilitating it used to be for you, and how hopeless you would feel. But now, I see that when the depression comes, it does not overwhelm you to desperation; however that is not enough. I want you to utterly and completely denounce this power over you that is not from Me! I **know** you have seen My hand in your life, and as you look back over nearly sixty years, you must see that I would never, *ever* leave you----you are My precious, child, and I love you with an everlasting love. You could never comprehend the depth, the height, the breadth of that love, because it is beyond your realm of understanding, but I want you to consider some evidences of the truth of My statement, so you will have proof of My love and My constant presence in your life.

     Whenever you feel the warmth of the sunlight on your skin, do you not know that it is Me touching you? When you see that certain color of blue sky that thrills you so, do you not know that it is I who designed that shade for your pleasure? And vibrant sunsets that bring you such enjoyment---they are My gift. Do you not see the graceful flight of My birds and butterflies and fail to recognize My desire to provide you with visual delights? And don't you know that I equipped the songbirds with varied trills for the sole purpose of being a gift for those who have ears to hear? When you walk in the woods or hike to a waterfall, do you not know that I share the silent smile in your heart? It pleases Me so, when you take the time to see and hear and taste and feel all I have provided. And when you recognize Me in My gifts, you and I are inextricably linked.

When you taste the varied flavors of the fruits I have set before you, don't you see My hand? When you bite into a juicy peach, a crunchy piece of celery, or a tender banana, do you not know that it is I who designed them to give you a full range of edible choices? Aren't you aware that I could have made all of them taste like *oatmeal* instead of providing a delight for your palate?

I did not create these visual, audible and taste sensations for *no purpose*! No, I wanted them to be evidence of the unfathomable depths of my care and concern for you! As you contemplate them, consider that if I care that much about your outward concerns, how much more I care about your *inner being*. With that in mind, can you comprehend what I want to convey about My everlasting love, My never-ending faithfulness, My constant care for you?

Don't you know that in times of need I am your Father, Brother, Husband, Friend when mere humans fail you? Think back to the crises in your life. Do you remember when you thought the floodwaters of despair would overcome you? Do you recall the times of desperation when you didn't think you could survive? *But you are still here. Who do you think preserved your life?* **Do you think I am no longer capable of such care?**

Do you not know that I have held you *always, in all ways,* in the palm of My hand? Have I not collected your tears in a bottle and dried your face with My tender touch? Can't you look back on My flawless record with assurance and KNOW beyond any shadow of a doubt that I will always be there, just as I have always been there in the past? And so, my child, I ask you to forsake this depressive temperment---to utterly and completely renounce its hold on you---trusting that it is My desire that you be healed of this debilitating self-defeating behavior.

It is not as if you have not known Me! Indeed, you have experienced Me walking with you throughout the years. Why, then, do you go back to this unproductive conduct like a dog goes back to its vomit? ENOUGH! Turn to Me---to Me only--and listen not to the false voice that says you are alone. You are not alone; you *never* have been! Now pick yourself up, turn to My Light, and walk confidently on My path. My Word is a lamp to your feet and a light unto your path; never forget that!

I speak to you in My Word, and I am ever-present in the praise you offer to Me. It is not as though you do not know how or where to find Me. Why do you not avail yourself of that knowledge? Sometimes you are like one who has a key to a beautiful palace, but stands outside in the rain bemoaning the fact that you are getting wet! You know Me---therefore stand on My promises. **Stand, I say!** *Stand firm*, knowing that it is I Who upholds you with My strong right hand. I do not ask you to stand on sinking sand; you are to stand on the Rock, recalling My promises:

*I will turn your mourning into dancing (Jeremiah 31:13)

*When you pass through the waters, I will be with you; and through the rivers, they shall not overflow thee. . .(Isaiah 43:2).

*You will not be tested beyond your strength; I will provide a way out so you may endure it (1 Corinthians 10:13).

*Be anxious for nothing; but in everything by prayer and supplication let your requests be made known unto God. And the peace of God, which passes all understanding, shall keep your heart and mind through Christ Jesus (Philippians 4:6-7).

*Be not crushed on their account; as though I would leave you crushed before them. . . (Jeremiah 1:17-19).

*Therefore the redeemed of the Lord shall return, and come with singing into Zion; and *everlasting joy* shall be upon their head; they shall obtain gladness and joy; and sorrow and mourning shall flee away (Isaiah. 51:11).

*By waiting and by calm shall you be saved; in quiet and trust your future lies (Isaiah 30:15).

*You shall not die but live, and declare the works of the Lord (Psalm 119:17).

By the way, this last word was given to you nearly four years ago, and still you have not embraced the full power of its promise!

You are My daughter, a child of the King. . .that makes you a princess! And it is unbefitting for a princess to moan and wail like a homeless waif who knows not her heritage!

I know My own, and My own know Me . . . now embrace My Truth, hold My hand, and walk with Me in assurance, in confidence, in peace, in comfort---in boldness. You are a child of the Promise, and I will *never* leave you!

Love from your Father,
Almighty God of the Universe, your Lord and Savior

My Lord, and my God!
I am overwhelmed! Forgive my lack of trust. Keep my mind stayed on You; be my strength and my guide when I stray from You.

Some years ago, You gave me a promise from Scripture to embrace: that You comfort me in all my tribulations, that I may be able to comfort them which are in any trouble, by the comfort which I myself received from You (2 Corinthians 1:3,4). I know that You keep in perfect peace those whose hearts are stayed on You, so I ask You to keep my heart and mind focused on You, that I may comfort others with the comfort which I myself have received from You!

Your loving and grateful daughter,
Arlene

In the Eye of the Storm

Sometimes, with the world swirling and twirling around us in a dispiriting storm, it seems like the last place one would choose to be is in the eye of the storm. But having been raised in South Florida---home of the hurricanes---I have learned that it is precisely *in* the eye of the storm that there is calm!

When it seems as though I can't see my hand in front of my face, much less the light at the end of the tunnel, I may be tempted to cry out to have the present difficulty or adversity removed. I have often prayed that the Lord would remove some desperate situation from me, and I know that is how many people turn to God. But I have lived through enough years to have finally come to an understanding that it is in the very storms of life that the Lord has dealt most effectively with me. Just as I experienced the annual threat of hurricanes, I learned through my own struggles that being in the eye of the storm is where there is calm and a sense of peace. When the storm is raging all around, being in the center---centered on the Lord---is the most comforting place to be.

The word of the Lord tells us to become as little children in our faith and trust, but that does not mean we are to become childish. For many years my prayer was a whining and petulant, "Do this, Lord" or "Do that." I shudder to think of how many times I acted like a spoiled brat, demanding that the Lord---the Creator God of the Universe, no less!---kowtow to my bidden wishes. Those were the days when instead of being child-like, I was being very, very childish.

But as I look back on my journey, I see that in the midst of the storms---right in the depth of the darkest moments---was truly when the Lord held me in the palm of His mighty Hand! Have you ever experienced, as the little saying by an anonymous author states, that "Sometimes God calms the storm; and sometimes He lets it rage, *and calms His child*"? Like most people who have read the inspirational story continained in "Footprints," I know that there were situations when I knew beyond a shadow of a doubt that I could absolutely not make it through . . .and yet, here I am. That is a testimony to the grace and mercy of God. He has been my Rock, my Provider, the Lifter of my head. And I stand in awe before the mighty God of the universe and confess that I among all people am least worthy of His ongoing and continuing love and care.

This book is not a chronological journal or autobiography. In fact, you will find that the stories swing back and forth between my years as a young adult, to being a wife and mother of babies, the mother of teens, and a grandmother. There will be times, no doubt, when you will wonder why the chronology jumped around so much, and why---just when you think you have the time-frame down pat---I leap backwards to a past era. I have no explanation. But if you have any comments to make, I suggest you take it up directly with the One Who inspired this collection. I finally tired of trying to "make sense" out of the pattern, and assume that the serious and the funny and the poignant stories are interwoven for a purpose.

There are many chapters of my life's journey and struggles that are not related here. This collection of stories is not an unveiling of all the intimate details of personal struggles, particularly those involving others. I don't believe in exposés or airing one's dirty laundry in public, but any woman who has been a mother, wife, daughter, sister, neighbor, co-worker, friend, knows that there are times of deep sorrow as well as joy in those relationships. There are times of disappointment, rejection, frustration and crushing hopelessness. This book is meant merely to encourage you, the reader, to examine your own life with new awareness of the lessons you have learned and the growth you have experienced as you walked across the mountains and through the valleys. Note that the Twenty-third Psalm says we will walk *through* the valley---we will not stay there. I think one of my favorite phrases in Scripture is "And it came to pass. . ." It *could* have said, "And it came to stay!"

As Iron Sharpens Iron, So Girls Sharpen Girls
(Proverbs 27:17)

New friendships are silver, but old friendships are gold, as the saying goes. How true! There's something about having weathered twenty or thirty years of friendship that is truly a precious gift.

When I was in my early twenties, I moved up to New York City, from my little hamlet in South Florida known as Coral Gables. Initially I lived with Aunt Jean and her family for a few weeks, but eventually another girl whom I knew from Florida decided to move up to New York, too. Doris was a stewardess, and in order to afford the big city rents we added a third roommate to the picture. We found a convenient apartment off Central Park West, across the street from the Museum of Natural History and the Planetarium. There was a subway at the corner, and busses on three of the streets within a block of our apartment.

Our humble abode was small---one bedroom with two twin beds, a living room with a sleeper/sofa, and a little kitchen, but there were three large closets, which were a must if three girls were to live together. And best of all, the building had a reception desk downstairs, and a central switchboard system, where an operator received all incoming calls. Clever young gals that we were, we soon figured out that we could have the switchboard operator "screen" our calls for us. If it was from someone we were anxiously awaiting a call from, "he" got through right away, but if it was someone we were trying to avoid, then the operator said we were out.

I had gotten a job in the steno pool of a large law firm of over a hundred lawyers. Back in Florida I had received some wonderful experience being the secretary to an attorney who was also a Commissioner, meaning he was at the Commission one day a week, leaving me to handle lots of assignments on my own. He had given me an exemplary letter of recommendation when I left, and after a few weeks at the New York law firm, I was offered the position of private secretary to one of the senior partners. Unfortunately, I was pretty naive and didn't realize that the steno pool wouldn't stand for "the new kid on the block" bucking the system like that, taking the job that they had already "designated" for one of their own.

Horrible rumors were spread about me, including that I had only gotten the job because I had "ingratiated myself" to the office manager. And in those days that was a polite way of saying what is not so politely said today. If you could ever have seen the office manager, you would know how ludicrous that rumor was. Nevertheless, I was the brunt of devastating innuendoes and slander and was shunned by almost the entire female staff. Each day I would go to work, holding my head up and trying to do my best to ignore the snubs, and each night I would go back to my apartment and cry. Doris told me to stop taking the guff and quit that job. But I was determined not to allow some narrow-minded gossip-mongers to dictate my life for me. It was doubly painful to stay, because the partner I was assigned to was an extremely difficult and demanding man to work for. Nevertheless, I prayed for strength and courage each day, and ended up working there for eight years! I grew up a lot, too, and learned lots more than secretarial skills.

But life had it brighter moments during that time, too. I loved the theatre and the wonderful musicals, and tried to take advantage of all that the Big Apple had to offer. Even back then, tickets to the Broadway shows were expensive and hard to get. However, if one timed it right, the best seats could be obtained at a rather low price. Doris and I would wait for a snowstorm--and a blizzard was even *better* insurance--to get into the shows we wanted to see for the price of Standing-Room-Only tickets! The only problem was that while we were in the theatre, the snow kept falling . . . and falling. . . and when the show was over there was virtually no way to get back home, because all transportation was at a standstill. We never let a little detail like *that* deter us, however; and we managed to see most all of the best shows during our years there.

At one time we were looking for a third roommate and were discussing some girls who might be possibilities. I was ironing and dressed in a nightgown, when suddenly I was startled as our apartment door flew open and a girl in a stewardess uniform---whom I had never seen before---put one foot inside our apartment, mumbled, "Ohhhhh . . . sorry!" and went back out, closing the door behind her. (Apparently she lived in the building and her key fit our door, too). Doris said she knew that the girl, whose name was Terri, wanted to find different roommates. And we figured as long as she already had a key to our apartment, she probably should be ours!

Terri always had a million questions---most of them about God. And most of them surfaced after midnight, when I was desperately trying to get a few hours of sleep before having to get up for work. I was the only one who had a regular 9-5 job as a legal secretary. So while she could sleep late, I had to get up early the next morning. Terri's questions started, "If God. . . , then why. . . . ?

Eventually all three of us married and went off to three different states to live. We each had children and raised them through all the joys and trials of parenting. We've kept in touch throughout all those years, and every so often we have a "reunion." And when we do, it's like old-times all over again.

I love planning reunions and surprises, and I have such fun thinking up ways to cram as much as possible into two or three days. The year we all turned fifty, we had our reunion in New York, and I called our old building manager---who was the same manager we'd had 25 years earlier. (And we thought he was an old man *back then!*) I asked if he remembered me and the girls from Apartment 1200, and he emphatically replied, "Yes I remember you! You're the ones who painted all the furniture black and the walls red!" (Well, he'd given us three different kitchen chairs, and we just sort of, well, "matched them up." And as for the red walls, *only two* of them were red. And it brightened up the place!) I wondered if I should hang up before he called the police, but I figured the statute of limitations had run out, so I ventured forth with the reason for my call.

I told him about our plans for a reunion and asked if he had an apartment available for the weekend we were planning. (It was a residential hotel, and some rooms and apartments were rented by the month; others by the night). I also said that while I knew that Apartment #1200 was probably not available, we'd love to have any

13

apartment with that same layout. He said he'd see what he could do. I was the first to arrive in New York (by car), and I went to the hotel to register. The desk clerk handed me a key and I looked at it and gasped, "Twelve Hundred? We're in TWELVE HUNDRED?!" The clerk thought perhaps I had an aversion to that number and said, "We can change the room for you if you'd like." I clasped the key tight and held it against my chest and said, "Oh, NO! This will be _just fine_, thank you!" (And thank YOU, Lord!)

I kept telling myself that I'd be very nonchalant when I drove out to the airport to pick up Doris and Terri later that afternoon, and not tell them that we'd gotten our very same ole apartment! It would be a surprise when they arrived. I brought my suitcase upstairs and then went back down to the local grocery for some picnic-fixings. There was a performance of Shakespeare's "Two Gentlemen From Verona" playing in the outdoor theater in Central Park that evening, and I knew the "girls" would love it! (Note: Women who have been friends from young adulthood up through grandparenthood are eternally known as "girls" to one another). After bringing the groceries up to the apartment, I set off for the airport for my unsuspecting friends arriving from two different states.

I'm not sure who won the squealing contest---actually I think it was a three-way tie! After reveling in the excitement of being back in our very own apartment---a feat probably none of us expected in our wildest dreams---we packed up our picnic, stripped one bed of a sheet to use for a tablecloth, and headed for the park. The performance was spectacular and we finished the evening with a horse-drawn carriage ride through the park and three gloppy desserts at the famous landmark, Lindy's.

The next day we raced to the Twofers Office (where you can get tickets for a Broadway matinee show for half-price, four hours before the scheduled performance). Tickets in hand, we went to the Metropolitan Museum of Art and then to lunch at a restaurant in Central Park before dashing to the theater. As soon as that show was over, we ran back to the Twofers Office for tickets to an evening performance of a second musical. Once again, with our tickets safely tucked away, we went to a small gallery for a special showing of a three-dimensional art display. We almost got "invited to leave" when we "interacted" a little too exhuberantly with some of the art, but "Fiftyish Girls Just Want to Have Fun. . ." After dinner and the theater, we walked all around town, ending up at Rockefeller Center for dessert. The next morning after we'd gone to church and had brunch together, I drove the girls back to the airport. I was filled with thanksgiving for the extraordinary visit we'd been granted.

A few years later we had another reunion, this time at the farm in Blairsville. I met the girls at the Atlanta airport and we stopped for dinner. An unexpected surprise awaited them, as I took them to an Elvis Presley (impersonator) concert and we laughed with reminiscence at the antics of the singer. Time for banana splits before heading to the farm, where we finally arrived well after midnight. If you recall Terri's penchant for lonnnng philosophical talks after midnight, then you know what we were in for! Finally, around 2:00 a.m., I said, "We **have** to go to sleep, because I have a full day planned for tomorrow!" Well, so much for my powers of persuasion---because just before 3:00 a.m., I finally conceded that it was going to be a lonnnnnnng night. I suggested that as long as we were still up, we should have breakfast while we talked, so when we finally *did* go to bed we could sleep in a little later in the morning. We fixed omelets and fruit and eventually got to bed at 3:30 a.m.!

Early the next morning (7:00 a.m.!), Terri was standing in my bedroom doorway saying, "Psssst, Arlene. Wake up." I opened one eye and asked, "Why?" Terri replied, "Because it's morning." I retorted, "Terri---it was morning when we went to bed! That's why we had breakfast, so we could sleep a little later!" I should've known better. There's no stopping that gal when she wants to talk!

Terri persisted, "Besides, you've been telling us you've been running this farm by yourself (while Bill is working in Florida), and I believed you." Me: "Sooooo?" Terri: "Well, I just looked out my bedroom window and saw the farmer out there." Me: "Really? What did he look like?" Terri: "Kind of Mexican, wearing a sort of serape and swinging a sickle in the tall grass." Me: "Ohhhh, uhmm,

15

yeah. Well, I *do* have a helper, but He's not exactly an earthly one."
Terri: "But I *saw* him!" Me: "Let's go look."

We went to the bedroom she was sharing with Doris (who was
still asleep), and looked out the window. Terri whispered: "He was
right *there* in the field!" My response was a smile. I suggested if we
were going to continue to talk, we go outside and not disturb Doris.
We put on warm robes, gathered up quilts and pillows and went out
to the hammock to talk. She asked me what it meant, and I said,
"The harvest is great but the laborers are few." I told her I believed
it was the Lord's challenge to her to be part of His harvesting. His
word says many are called, but few are chosen, and it seemed He had
sent out a personally engraved invitation to Terri to be part of His
Grand Plan.

As I wrote this story about the sickle and the harvest, I decided
to look up the word "sickle" in my Concordance. I wanted to see the
context in which it was used in the Bible. I found a powerful reading
in Revelation 14:15-20. I wonder if I may have missed the true
meaning of Terri's vision the first time around, and if it was perhaps
a word of instruction for us about the day of judgment? If so, the
Lord will clear up the confusion; He is the God of order!

As for me, I am grateful to the Lord for the girls like Doris
and Terri, whom He used to "grow me up" and with whom I continue
to stretch and grow. We pull and push one another with a sense of
holy awe for the personhood of the other and I believe I speak for
each of us when I say that whenever we meet--in person, by phone or
by letter--we are filled anew with gratitude for the gift of friendship
and comraderie we continue to share even after all the years that have
passed. It was no "coincidence" that Terri's key fit our apartment
door!

... And a Little Child Shall Lead Them

No matter how "wise" or well-intentioned any parent may be, there are occasions when there is overwhelming evidence to support the theory that "out of the mouths of babes" comes a wisdom that truly cannot be denied. For example, when our youngest child, Scott, was about seven, he expressed the desire to be a doctor---a pediatrician, to be specific. He wanted to go to poor countries and help the children where there were no doctors. His aspirations pleased me, and I continued the discussion by explaining that doctors are "partners" with God, and that it was He who did the healing.

Scott acknowledged that he knew that. I continued, "It's sort of like that bumper sticker that says: 'God is my co-pilot'." A look of consternation crossed his little face, and I noticed that he seemed a bit confused. He replied, "That's not right."

I was stunned. Where had I gone wrong? I had always tried to teach my children a proper relationship with the Lord, and here was Scott telling me that God was not his co-pilot! Now it was my turn to register confusion and consternation. I tried to explain it another way. "You know, Scott, it's like co-chairmen or co-partners or co-workers."

He seemed even more determined as he repeated, "But God is not my co-pilot." After a pause he continued, "He is the pilot and I am *His* co-pilot!"

My eyes grew wide with a renewed understanding, and my eyes filled with tears of wonder at the way the Lord teaches us lessons, even those of us who consider ourselves "teachers." It was a humbling but beautiful example of how a little child is often used to lead and confound the proud. It brought back to my recollection two incidents in which I saw a little child change a somewhat hardened heart. Both took place before I was married, in two very different settings.

During the years I worked in New York City, I volunteered at the Foundling Hospital (a temporary home for orphaned children). Every Sunday for five years, I could be found in the ward with the children aged 18 months to 3 years. It didn't matter if it was my birthday, Easter Sunday, or Christmas; if it was a Sunday, I was surrounded with children hungrily seeking attention. There was one special child who captured my heart: 3-year-old José, with his big, dark eyes and long black lashes. We had a special love-bond between us. Occasionally on a Saturday I would take him out for the day and together we would discover the wonders the city had to offer---the museums, Central Park, the zoo, etc.

One day while we were in Central Park, José saw a man selling balloons and ran over to him. I let him choose whatever color he wanted, and he got a big yellow one. He was so excited! He wanted to tell the world that Mommy Arlene had bought him a yellow balloon! Suddenly I heard a voice behind me say in a surprised voice, "*Miss* Edwards, he is *yours*?" I wheeled around to see one of the senior partners from the law firm where I worked, pushing a very elegant shiny black English pram with a beautiful satin and lace comforter covering a young baby. (In 1960 it would have been grounds for dismissal if an unmarried woman was known to have a baby out-of-wedlock, and to add fuel to the fire, José was a dark-skinned Hispanic child and I was a green-eyed blonde). In answer to his question, I replied softly, "Oh, that he were! But he's mine for *today*, Mr. Barber. I volunteer at the Foundling Hospital and I can take him out occasionally." Although the attorney had a reputation for being rather stern, his face softened as we spoke, and his voice became far more gentle than anyone in the firm had ever heard him speak. From that day on he always went out of his way to greet me and inquire about José and the children at the Foundling.

Another time I took petite little Nilsa (24-months-old, but still in size 15-month clothing) out for the day to see the Christmas decorations. As we got off the escalator in Macy's, she wrenched loose from my hand and disappeared into the crowd. I was frantic, and it was nearly a full minute before I spotted her. (Sixty seconds in such a situation is interminable!) When I did find her, she had approached a man making a purchase and had grabbed him around

18

the knees from behind, saying, "Dad-dee, dad-dee!" The man was in his late 50's and was clearly incensed and agitated by the scene. (Nilsa was also a dark-skinned, black-haired little child, and the man was a burly construction worker-type Caucasian.) As I approached, I scooped her up into my arms and apologized profusely to the man. "I'm so sorry," I said. "She doesn't see men very often, and I apologize for the incident." He gave me a very judgmental look and wanted to know why she didn't see men, so I explained, "She's from the Foundling Hospital and the only men there are the occasional handymen and janitors. She doesn't get out too frequently and has a limited vocabulary. Women are 'mommy,' and men are 'daddy.' Please forgive us for the inconvenience."

Once again I saw a stone-faced facade crumble as the man reached out and took Nilsa into his own arms. He said, "I'm a bachelor. I've never had any children of my own." And then the mist in his eyes and the catch in his throat overcame him. I watched as he allowed himself to be transformed into a kind, caring and gentle man and was reminded once again of the power of a child.

In both circumstances there were only momentary incidents that impacted those men. And yet, I believe they were touched in ways that they rarely had been before. Lord, I pray that You will keep my own heart open and humble and my eyes and ears attuned in childlike wonder to see and hear the lessons You have for me!

Ladies & Gentlemen, Please Be Seated!

I reckon I was "before my time." Even when I was only in my early twenties, I already had a sense of adventure and a feeling of wonder about the marvelous world about me and the incredible Creator who had fashioned it. In 1960, it was not customary for a young woman to travel alone--particularly to foreign countries. But after travelling with a church youth group on a guided tour of Europe when I was 21, I decided I had learned enough to be my own tour guide the second time I went. So, just before my 23rd birthday, I took a charter flight to Europe in order to meet my roommate Doris for two weeks of touring. Unfortunately, the charter flight was scheduled six days prior to Doris' vacation, so I had some time on my hands.

During the flight, I talked with several passengers, and they all had very definite plans and one or more travelling companions. There were three of us, however, who didn't know anyone else on the flight (or each other, for that matter). It was a year during which the Oberammergau Passion Play in Germany was presented---an event that occurs only every ten years, and which is usually sold out a year in advance. Since the 1500's, and originating during a time of plague, all the citizens of that little hamlet in the Bavarian alps have participated in an enormous production every decade, in thanksgiving to God for sparing their village. The production is presented for three months in the summertime, and lasts from 9:00 a.m. until 6:00 p.m., with a two-hour lunch break. I had a burning desire to see the play, even though I had been unsuccessful in getting a ticket for it.

The two other solo-travelers were a fireman and a construction worker. I tried to convince them that the Passion Play would be a once-in-a-lifetime event, and I knew they would love it! (They were equally convinced that they would absolutely not love it, and it was their last choice on their non-existent agenda). Nevertheless, at the end of the ten-hour flight, since they had no other plans, they reluctantly agreed to travel to Oberammergau.

The charter flight landed in Paris, and we had to take a series of trains into the Bavarian countryside. After two days of travelling, we arrived at the ticket office just as the day's performance had begun and were told that there were no tickets available. (During the entire trip, my two reluctant fellow travelers had bemoaned the fact that we were probably on a wild-goose chase, and now they were smugly--but sadly--saying, "I told you so!") I silently asked the Lord to open a door for us, even though it seemed futile. I expressed my deep disappointment to the ticket-seller, and finally he said, "If you come back during the lunchbreak, I'll see if there is anything available." So we spent some time sightseeing around the quaint little village and had lunch, and I silently implored the Lord to help us to see this phenomenal production.

Just before time to go back to the ticket office, I excused myself to go to the ladies' room downstairs at a hotel, and the two fellows waited outside. As I entered the restroom, I passed a woman washing her hands, and in the stall there was a Chinese coolie-hat hanging on the back of the door. I called out, "Excuse me, is this your hat?" In a British accent, she replied, "Yes, it is." I passed the hat over the door and she left. As I approached the sink, I saw a diamond ring and knew it had to have been hers. I went upstairs to the conceirge at the hotel desk and turned the ring in to him. By the time I went outside, the fellows had gotten concerned about my extended absence and thought perhaps I had become ill. I told them that I had found a diamond ring, and they exclaimed, "What a stroke of luck! That will pay for your whole trip to Europe!" I explained that I had turned the ring in to the conceirge. "What did you do *that* for?" "Well," I said, "it didn't belong to me, and it needs to be returned the woman who lost it." They couldn't believe it. Their expression told me they wouldn't have turned it in.

As we headed to the ticket office, I felt very uncertain about the conceirge's integrity and announced to the fellows, "I can't go to the ticket office; I have to go to the police station." They were incredulous. We had travelled for two days, and here we were on the verge of possibly receiving tickets for the play--and I wanted to go to the police station! While we were at the station, a policeman was dispatched to the hotel and returned with the ring. When I was satisfied that I had done all I could do, we left to see if there were any seats for us.

The second half of the play was just about to begin, and the man at the ticket booth had a big smile on his face. "I have seats for you," he said. *Halleluia!* He had arranged for three folding chairs to be put in the aisle, and in that huge amphitheatre seating over 4,000 people, there was no one blocking our view! Once seated, I was still troubled and I silently implored the Lord, "You know me, Lord. And you know that I will not be able to give the play my full attention unless I know that woman got her ring back. Please give me a sign to reassure me." Suddenly, right down the very aisle where we were seated (even though there were half a dozen aisles) came a woman with a Chinese coolie-hat on her shoulders! I stood up and called, "Excuse me, did you get your ring back?" And in that same crisp British accent came the reply, "Yes, I did." I was ecstatic!

Afterwards the fellows admitted that the Passion Play was truly a very moving experience and they said they were glad they had seen it. (I knew they'd be touched). Following the performance we went our separate ways, and I headed back to Paris to await Doris' arrival two days after I got there. The next time I saw those young men was the day we arrived at the airport for the charter flight back to the U.S. They told me about some of the things they had seen and done, but conceded that the Passion Play was one of the highlights of their trip and they were glad I had insisted on going to see it. They may have been "reluctant" when we began, but the visible and moving dramatization of Jesus' life, death and resurrection had made an impact on them. I never saw them again, and I often prayed that there were other seeds that had been sown in their lives to bring them to a relationship with the real-life Person who had laid down His life for them, that they might have life and have it to the full!

Thou Hast Put Gladness In My Heart

After thinking about all fun times we'd had during our reunions, I recalled another time Terri and I had gotten together that was worthy of a "story." She and her family were going to be driving southeast from Kansas to attend a wedding. My family was going to be driving northwest from Florida in the motorhome on vacation. Hmmm, southeast/northwest . . .sounds like we ought to be able to make a connection *somewhere!* I pored over the maps until I found a spot where our paths might cross, and we made reservations to meet at a motel at the intersection of I-24 and S.R. 231 in Tennessee at a town neither of us had heard of before: Murfreesboro. We planned to meet at noontime, so we could spend the day together, let the children swim in the pool, have dinner, and then go our own ways the next day after breakfast.

On the day of our appointed meeting, we were travelling at a good pace, but then we got caught in some unexpectedly heavy accident-related traffic. We lost nearly an hour, and I was feeling frustrated at the "stand-still." (If the sin of pride raises its ugly little head in my life, it's when I think I've planned something "perfectly," and it doesn't turn out as expected). We still had nearly two hours to travel, and we were going to be an hour late! Suddenly we approached a glorious sign: "Entering Central Time Zone." We got to adjust our clocks back one hour! *That meant we were going to be right on time after all.*

When we arrived at the motel, Terri & Co. were already in bathing suits enjoying the pool. It didn't take us long to join them. We spent a pleasant, lazy afternoon and enjoyed the antics of the "human ice-cream sundae" as they climbed on each other's shoulders, three-high, with little six-year old Scott becoming the fourth and final member as "the cherry on the top!" Later we got cleaned up for dinner at a lovely restaurant and after the children were tucked in bed for the night, the adults sat outside our rooms overlooking the pool and gabbed. . . . and gabbed. . . . .and gabbed.

We had adjoining rooms at the motel, and the next morning--- EARLY the next morning---I sensed something (perhaps a puppy?) next to my bed. It was no puppy; it was that scalawag, Terri, on hands-and-knees, peering into my bleary eyes. "Get up," she said. So I got up, dressed and met her out on the deck near the pool. We talked for a long time and realized we were getting hungry. Since our husbands and children were still sound asleep, we thought we'd drive over to the nearby waffle-shop and have some breakfast. After we'd been there more than an hour, lingering over coffee while we caught up with one another's lives, we looked out and saw a straggly band of two men and five children approaching the restaurant.

To this day we look back in amazement that with all the color-coded clothing we had packed, how it was possible to *mis*-match the children's apparel in such a discordant fashion! We agreed to pretend we didn't see them, or at least that we didn't *know* them. But Terri's husband, unshaven, and playing the part to the hilt, walked over to our table and in a sad, hang-dog way, said in a loud stage whisper for all to hear, "The children have really missed you." They then walked to a large table in the back of the restaurant--and we thought about crawling under our table. A few minutes later, as my husband Bill was cutting up waffles for the children, the knife, the waffle and the plate went in three different directions and the plate crash-landed on the floor in a dozen pieces. There was a moment of hushed silence, followed by the squeaky voice of a six-year-old asking, "Do we have to pay for the plate now, *too*, Daddy?" That was our cue to beat a path to the door, and when we asked for our check the waitress said it had been paid for by the men at the table in back. We told her, "They're probably just looking for someone to look after their children, but we're not going to fall for that!" The look on her face as we left was priceless, and she's probably still trying to figure out that scenario.

It was a short visit that included three meals: hamburgers out by the pool, a lovely dinner and a leisurely breakfast. We had been fed once again by the bounty of the Lord, both physically and---more importantly---spiritually. I know that my life is richer, sweeter, more joy-filled when I drink deeply from the communion cup of friendship that the Lord provides.

The Bible tells us "there is a time to weep and a time to laugh," and Psalm 4:7 says, "Thou has put gladness in my heart." We are told that Jesus came that we might have life and have it to the full---abundant life. There are promises that our mourning will be turned to dancing; that a glad heart lights up the face; and that a merry heart is the health of the body. And I believe that the Lord loves to laugh with us when we recognize and delight in the blessings He has given us.

Speak, Lord, Your Servant is Listening
-vs-
Listen, Lord, Your Servant Is Speaking

There are times when I know I am being led by the Lord, and other times when I don't seek His guidance and go off on my own. The results are quite different, and occasionally even disastrous, as this story illustrates.

Friends are a gift from God. In my case, having had no sisters, they provide a special relationship that is lacking in my life. Have you ever unwittingly jeopardized a friendship and watched as the light goes out in your once-close friend's eyes? I have been guilty of such transgressions. And I have suffered the grievous loss of closeness because of my impulsivity and lack of discernment.

While living in New York, I found a good friend in Marti. She called one day and asked me to meet her for dinner about something important. She told me she had just discovered that she was adopted. She was feeling hurt and bewildered. Nevertheless, after reflecting on it for a few days, she said she had absolutely no interest in locating her natural parents. And for about thirty years, that's how the situation stood.

Even after I moved back to Florida and 1,400 miles separated us, we maintained a close friendship. One day I received a call from her and she said there was a group that helped adoptees find their birth roots. She was going to pursue it. A few short months later, they had matched her up with some names and locations of her birth mother and her birth father. Marti wrote a discreet letter in order not to put her mother in a compromising position, in case she was married and her husband didn't know about a previous pregnancy. No response. She wrote again a while later. Again, no response.

Then I got a rather despondent early morning call from Marti, bemoaning the fact that while she might have somehow understood the abandonment by her mother when she was a young, unmarried girl, this was truly a rejection by a mature woman who was willfully rejecting and renouncing her relationship to Marti. She was crying, and it was not something she did often. I was distressed. "Coincidentally," while Marti lived in New York City, her birth mother worked only about ten miles away from me in Ft. Lauderdale!

After our telephone conversation ended, I wished I could somehow get Marti and her mother together. So, without checking it out with the Lord, I headed for the office where Marti's mother worked. At first, her mother thought *I* was "Marti," and she looked as frightened as a trapped deer looking down the barrel of a rifle, but I told her I was not who she thought I was, but merely an emissary on her behalf. She told me she had legal rights to privacy and that she had a new life/husband and did not want to jeopardize that. I told her what a wonderful person Marti is: kind, sensitive, caring. I told her about the years of volunteer work she was involved in; I described Marti's children, and she was surprised to learn that she was a grandmother. (She'd never had any children other than Marti). At the end, I extended my hand and she placed hers in mine as I said, "I believe if we had met under other circumstances, you and I would like one another, and I *know* you would like Marti!" A shy smile came across her face and she said, simply, "Perhaps." I was puffed up with the feeling that progress had been made.

That night I couldn't wait to call Marti. I was so excited. It hadn't dawned on me that I had violated a serious breach of confidence. Marti had told me never to contact her mother, and I had agreed to that stipulation. But that morning when she cried, I threw that promise to the winds and let myself be guided by my own self-centered beliefs that I could make something good happen. Unfortunately, not only did something good NOT happen; but something very destructive did happen. Marti lost confidence in me and my pledge of confidentiality. All my protestations that "I didn't care anything about being the one who met your mother first" merely served as evidence of my justifying unacceptable behavior.

For several years, our friendship suffered a severe rift; a chasm that neither of us seemed to be able to bridge. It was a difficult time for both of us, I believe. But for me it was intolerable. I realized that I had crossed a line in the sand, and there was no taking it back. What was done was done. And all because I had not checked it out with the Lord, but had instead raced pell-mell straight into danger.

But God is the Lord of forgiveness, of pardon, of reconciliation. In time, He healed our hearts and reunited two broken spirits into His spirit. And through it all, He taught me a valuable lesson. It is better to seek God's face FIRST and get your marching orders, than to try to slay the dragon single-handedly!

Send In the Clowns!

If you've ever experienced a situation in which you considered yourself in over your head, then you'll be able to identify with this story.

During a church fair many years ago, I was working in the face-painting booth---thinking how much fun it was painting a heart or a rainbow or a smiley-face on little children and watching as their faces lit up like a Christmas tree and burst into big grins. Some of the children wanted a symbol representing a favorite sports team or a pet or a flower, and I was feeling somewhat smug about my artistic talents (limited as they are) and being able to fulfill their requests.

I even convinced a few adults to let me put a little drawing on their cheek and enjoyed seeing the childlike attitude that transformed them as they joined the youngsters in a light-hearted evening.

Then, a man I never saw before came into the booth and said he wanted a full clown face. It was a somewhat unusual request, but I reached for the white face paint and asked him what kind of clown he'd like to be. I thought I detected the smell of liquor on him, and I was beginning to wonder what this was all about. In answer to my question about what kind of clown face he wanted, he replied, "Give me a happy face so I can pretend I have something to smile about."

As I slathered white face paint across his face, I said, "Awww, it couldn't be as bad as all that, could it?"

"Yes, it could," he replied and then paused. "My only son--17 years old--was killed in a motorcycle accident two weeks ago." And so saying, a solitary tear rolled down the white paint on his cheek..

I wanted to be out of there. I felt terribly inadequate to speak to this man in the midst of his pain. (Bear in mind that when you are putting make-up on another person, you're in much closer proximity than you would be in normal conversational situations, and as I held this stranger's chin in one hand and applied make-up with the other, he and I were inextricably "connected" with gossamer threads as the scenario unfolded.) As I continued to work on his make-up, I prayed that the Lord would release me from this situation.

I told him how terribly sorry I was, and I know he could feel my sympathy. He asked if I were a "believer" and I said that I was. But he quickly said he could never believe in God again. I told him that the Lord was grieving as much as he was in this situation, and that if he would let Him, the Lord would hold him together as he walked through this impossible valley.

I started to say, "If you had known you were only going to have your son for seventeen years . . ." but he interrupted me with an adamant, "**I would *never* have had him**!" Then the floodgates opened, the tears gushed forth, and he sobbed unabashedly.

There was a moment or two of awkward silence (because I thought I was supposed to say something. I hadn't recognized that the Lord was working in this matter and He didn't require *my* "wisdom," just my willingness to be His comforting hands). I became aware that I hadn't stopped working on his make-up during this time, and I was struck by how incredibly gentle my hands had seemed and how soft and pliable his face felt. After what seemed to be an interminable time, he spoke again. "No," he reflected, "that's not true. I wouldn't have missed knowing him for *anything*."

And suddenly a completely different demeanor overcame him. Even behind the clown make-up he seemed calm-- peaceful almost-- and not at all like he had looked (was it just minutes?) earlier. He bent over, kissed me gently on my cheek and softly said, "thank you."

After he had left, I stood there wondering how many people seeing the man with the full clown-face would have any idea of the miraculous transformation and healing that had occurred. On the outside, they may have only seen a "clown." But he and I both knew that the Lord had been working on him on the <u>inside</u>, where the real change had taken place.

I stood watching him disappear into the crowd and prayed, "Lord, forgive me for asking to be removed from this situation. Help me to learn that you never ask anything more of me than simply to be obedient and provide an opportunity for your grace to work."

Jesus Is My Light . . .And My Lighthouse!

For much of my child-rearing years, I was a "professional volunteer," which afforded me the opportunity of experiencing many diverse challenges that an employer would not have entrusted to me. For example, I had absolutely no accounting skills (in truth, whenever my checkbook reconciliations became too out of line, I'd simply close the account and open a new one at a different bank). This didn't deter the Plantation Junior Woman's Club from endowing me with the position of Chairman of Decorations for its annual Charity Fund-Raiser, the year it had a Caribbean Islands theme.

As Decorations Chairman I was given a "budget," a concept I had vaguely heard about but didn't quite understand. My budget for decorating the War Memorial Auditorium (a <u>huge</u> barn of a building) was $300. It probably would have taken twenty times that amount to do a reasonable job. I likened the situation to that of feeding the 5,000 with five loaves and two fish!

I asked the Lord how this job could possibly be accomplished. "What is free or cheap, Lord?" Well, in South Florida, there's the sky, the sun, the beach. Hmmmm, the beach----there's the sand and shells. In an inspired vision, I saw a lighthouse covered with sea-shells, and praised the Lord for His creative touch. I sketched it out to share with the Show Chairmen, who were equally excited.

If we used inverted cylindrical cardboard popcorn boxes as the base and covered them with a cement mix, we could imbed the seashells into the damp cement. We could cut a small door out of woodgrain contact-paper, and I recalled that the little individual sizes of ice cream in plastic containers that I bought for my children could serve as the dome on top of the lighthouse. There were lots of thick pieces of styrofoam in the Club's warehouse, which we could break into irregular shapes to represent islands for the lighthouses to sit on, and by gluing a flat piece of cardboard that would extend out from under the styrofoam, we would have a platform to make "waves" out of cement, lapping up onto the "islands." If we could find a small battery and bulb, we could even have *lighted* lighthouses! Having lighted centerpieces would allow us to dim the overhead lighting and make the huge auditorium seem more cozy and intimate.

When it was time for my committee of twelve members to meet, I told them to pack a picnic lunch and to wear bathing suits, and their children were welcome to come, too. ***Bathing suits?!*** Our first two meetings were held at the beach, where we collected over 14,000 small shells. We had to make 140 lighthouses for the table centerpieces, and each one required about 100 shells. One of the girls said her brother-in-law was an electrician; therefore the problem of wiring the batteries and bulbs together was solved.

I asked the local movie theatre if they would sell us empty popcorn containers, but they said they would have to charge me the price of a full carton of popcorn, because their bookkeeping balanced by counting their receipts *and* the empty cartons to see if the numbers correlated. There's no way we could afford that! So at the end of the day I went to the theatre with a flashlight and asked if I could look for empty cartons under the seats. They were greasy and I only found about ten cartons. Lord, please open a door for us to find clean, empty cartons. I finally located a distributor who allowed us to buy the cartons at cost, since it was for charity. We were on our way to becoming lighthouse engineers!

We still had to decorate the lobby and the walls of the "dinner-theatre" and once again I sought direction from the Lord. Something else that was "free or cheap"---(my criteria for this project)---was large sheets of colorful tissue paper. The Lord let me envision large "baskets" of brightly-colored flowers, and I knew that we could easily make large flowers out of the tissue paper. I wondered what we could use for "baskets," which I thought needed to be about four feet high by about three feet wide. We cut burlap into long strips, 3" wide and then lightly painted the long edges black. We wove the burlap into a "basket-weave" and formed them over semi-circles of chicken wire. (One of the members of the committee had a ranch, and we acquired chicken wire at my specified cost---free!)

Also, we thought that the centerpieces were attractive enough for us to sell at the end of the evening, and so our "impossible $300 budget" not only was sufficient, but we actually *made a profit* on the decorations that year. The Lord blessed the project by multiplying and returning to us the small amount of assets we had, full measure, pressed down and overflowing! I now see that it pleases Him to have us go to Him for help and direction FIRST, at the beginning of a project. And I am convinced that at those times that I didn't receive help from His storehouse of creative genius, it was because I failed to ask. (*"Ye have not because ye ask not."*)

Two years later, with even less credentials for running an organization which operated on an annual budget of about $50,000 (most of which was raised for distribution to charities), I became the president of this group. "Lord, did You notice that I only have a high-school diploma under my belt?! Surely there are others far more qualified and able. Where's Aaron!" Despite my reluctance, I assumed the club's leadership, bearing feelings of insecurity for the task that lie ahead. I often forget that it is by the Lord's strength and might that I am empowered, and I do not have to lean on my own understanding.

When that year's Charity Show was presented, I was the representative who officially welcomed the guests at the beginning of the show, and thanked them for their attendance and support at the end. There were two performances each year. I've already described the dinner-theater evening which was held the second night of the show. However, on the opening night, the seats were set up like a theater, and all the charities we supported and their clients were invited to be our guests. They included physically- and mentally-handicapped children and adults, and they comprised about ten percent of our theater-night audience.

Since I was dressed in a long formal evening gown and was the last person on stage giving closing remarks to the audience, I was pretty easy to spot when we all left the building. While waiting outside with my children as Bill went to get the car, a group of cerebral-palsied clients were gathered nearby. I asked if they had enjoyed the show, and with their charming childlike exuberance they started exclaiming, "It was wonderful!" "I liked it!" "You were great!" (and the comment that kept me most humble---said in one breath: "You-were-the-best-one/were-you-in-the-show?") There was a lot of slurring and blurry speech, but their comments were heartfelt and sincere. They reached out to touch my children, who sort of recoiled and hid behind my skirt. I explained that the people just wanted to touch them because they were my children and they recognized me.

Just then a van pulled up to the curb bearing a printed message on the side door, "This Van Courtesy of the Plantation Junior Woman's Club." I pointed it out to the children and asked, "Did you see that sign?" They had seen it, but didn't know what it meant. I told them that the proceeds of the Charity Shows were distributed to several organizations which worked with handicapped people, and those funds enabled them to have equipment or supplies they needed. Their response was three wide-eyed little faces and the words, "I didn't know *that*!" I asked them why they thought we did the Show each year, and they said, "Because we thought you liked to dance!" Lord, help me to keep asking questions so that I will know if my children understand the underlying reasons for the actions I take.

And Lord, please also remind me over and over that You are the One who illuminates my path if I just seek You! Thanks for the beautiful lighthouses, oh Lord of Light!

Surprises Unlimited!

Each person has certain gifts or talents. I think I got the talent for planning successful surprise parties. I believe that God wants us to celebrate special occasions and commemorate milestones in our lives. And if a surprise for the celebrant is included---it is the icing on the cake.

Once in a while, however, the surprise that I thought was for others is *on me*. There was that time I wanted to give my parents a big surprise party for their 25th anniversary. I was in New York City at the time, and they were in Florida. For months in advance I did all kinds of planning and arranging, and when I went home for Christmas (which was a few days before their anniversary), I said that since I was in my mid-20's, I'd like to have an afternoon open house party for my friends, without my parents being there---as though they were chaperones. My dad was quite miffed, but I said that after I had entertained my friends on my own for a while (say from 2-4 p.m.) I'd like for them to come home for the last part of the party and meet my friends. They reluctantly went to a movie and came back about 4:00-ish.

My mom got out of the car and reached the front steps first, and when she opened the door my dad saw her backing out of the house saying, "No....no...." He thought one of my friends had offended or hurt her (although they had never given him cause to suspect that), and he went charging up the steps. When he realized it was a surprise party for them, tears formed in his eyes. I was thrilled that I had been able to pull off such a successful surprise 25th anniversary party, but then I found out *why* they hadn't suspected---and the joke was on me. It was only their twenty-fourth anniversary! We had a lot of laughs over that, and it probably was one of the most successful "25th Anniversary" surprise parties ever!

Another time I realized that our family was going to celebrate three milestones within a few weeks of one another. I thought I might be able to pull off a triple-header, but it was going to take a lot of coordination and timing. The three events were my mother's 70th birthday, Bill's 50th birthday, and Bill Jr.'s 16th birthday. Each one knew I was in the midst of preparations for a surprise party---but I told each that it was for one of the others.

We had all of my Mom's guests park their cars at a nearby ballfield where they were met by my brother George and transported by a "trolley" to our house. Bill's guests and Bill Jr.'s guests were both told to park at a nearby duck pond. Mom thought the party was for Bill Jr., so when she arrived, we ushered her into the front room to distract her from all the decorations in the back area which would have tipped her off. The trolley pulled up to the house right on cue, looking rather out of place on our quiet residential street. I looked out and said, "I wonder what that is?" We went outside and Mom was shocked to discover the trolley was filled with all her friends.

I brought out some trays of hors d'oeuvres and cold drinks and said we were all going for a ride on the trolley. Bill and Billy both demurred, one saying he'd stay and see to the trays of food in the oven and the other saying he'd be "embarrassed" if his friends saw him in the trolley. I insisted: "It's your mother-in-law's (or grandmother's) birthday, and we're ALL going!" Off we went on a ride through the neighborhood.

When we got to the duck pond, we slowed near a group of people and Bill was surprised that they were all friends of ours. (He later said he wondered how come they were having a party and we hadn't been invited.) Everyone had balloons, and as Bill stood with his mouth wide open, they all got on the trolley, too, calling out "Surprise!" Billy peeked out the window and found himself looking straight into the eyes of *his* friends! Since there wasn't enough room in the trolley for everyone, we left Billy and the teens at the park for a few minutes with a cooler of drinks and chips, and brought the adults back to the house for lunch.

George accompanied the trolley driver back to the duck pond, and picked up the teens to bring them to Chuck E. Cheese's, where they had pizza and played games for a couple of hours. On the way back, the trolley driver stopped at the bakery and picked up the big sheet cake I had ordered that said:

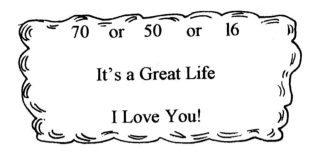

70 or 50 or 16

It's a Great Life

I Love You!

After a half-dozen hugs from my usually undemonstrative teen, who kept asking, "How, just *HOW* did you do this?" we all enjoyed cake and ice cream together, then one last trolley ride while gifts were opened. Everyone had a wonderful time. In fact, the trolley driver said it was the most fun he'd ever had with the trolley. It was a party that we still enjoy remembering.

For my mother's 80th birthday, I knew we were going to have to come up with something to top the trolley! We needed to launch a Grand Plan! I told Mom that my daughter and her family would be in town for a job interview and that while Keith was being interviewed I wanted to have a professional photograph taken of the four generations of women in our family. I said that afterward the four of us would meet Bill, Keith and baby Brandon (whom Bill was babysitting), and we'd all go out to dinner to celebrate her birthday. In actuality, my brother and I had rented one deck of a dinner-cruise boat, and since lots of folks love my mom, it wasn't hard to gather fifty relatives and friends from four states to join in the festivities. We made sure all the guests knew to get on board early, and we pulled up to the boat just moments before it was scheduled to depart. As we entered the deck filled with all her friends, neighbors, relatives and former co-workers, she was shocked and speechless. It was wonderful to be part of such a joyous occasion. That birthday cake had 24 "carrots" on it and said "Happy Birthday to a 24-carrot Lady!" (And in addition to warm memories of a great party, I have a beautiful keepsake portrait of four generations.)

43

I never cease to be amazed at how smoothly the surprises have turned out, and I know it is because the hand of the Lord was on them. He loves to see His children celebrating His goodness, His bounty, and His provision. He came that we might have life and have it to the full. And He loves you. *Surprise!*

God Resides *Where?*

After hearing a particularly touching and meaningful teaching one Sunday, I was so moved that I bought copies of the audiotape. I planned to send them to friends to whom I thought the message would minister.

A few days later, before I had mailed the tapes, I decided to listen to them again. I put one in my cassette player and listened as I did some housework. It was a good message, a sound teaching, a valuable lesson. . .but somehow it didn't impact me as being as life-changing or earth-shattering as I had remembered it the first time.

I was puzzled. I asked the Lord why I had thought the message was so dynamic and compelling earlier. His explanation was clear and explicit. It was because the first time I heard the message, it had been preceded by thirty minutes of praise and worship during which I had been completely immersed in adoration and reverence of the Lord. Therefore, when the teaching began, my spirit had been prepared and the message was received *in my heart*. However, the second time I heard it, I was listening somewhat distractedly as I worked, and the message was received solely *by my ears*. Whew!

It reminded me of an incident some time earlier when I had asked the Lord the meaning of the phrase in Scripture, "God inhabits the praise of His people." He had said, "If you are seeking Me, you will find Me in praise. That is where I dwell, where I reside." I hadn't fully understood His explanation at that time, but this surely cleared up any lack of understanding!

Lord, don't let me forget to prepare myself with an attitude of praise and worship, so that I may hear you with my heart, and not only with my ears. One is like strawberry shortcake, and the other is like dry crusty bread by comparison.

Recollections and Remembrances

If those of us who are parents (and particularly mothers) would be truthful, we'd have to admit that, despite our desire to claim otherwise, our children grew *us* up! Looking back over my life, I can trace those times when I became aware that each person is created individually with gifts, aptitudes, talents and skills that are uniquely their own. For example, just hours after each of my childrens' births, even if I had been blind, I could have told the difference between them by the way each laid in my arms and by the special way each one cried. And I think most mothers could claim the same.

I remember the year that Scott was born in the wee hours of Christmas Eve. The next day I was so anxious to get back home to be with Bill and the two other children, that I said to the doctor, "I *have* to go home. If the baby can't be released from the hospital he can stay another day, but I'm going!" The hospital packed Scott in a large Christmas stocking but he was still rolled tight into a fetal position and sank down to the bottom. At home, we put the new babe in his big stocking under the Christmas tree. I said to 15-month old Christy, "Remember that you wanted a baby-doll for Christmas? Well, here he is!" Little did I think that she would *believe* that. But when she was about three, I said to her, "Christy, I love watching you with Scott. You are very kind and patient with him, and you show him pictures in books and share so nicely." She said, "Well, he's mine." "Yes," I replied, "he's your brother." Big tears formed in her eyes and started cascading down her cheeks. "You <u>said</u>, he was *mine!*" About that time, big tears formed in my eyes as well. The extraordinary love of a child for her little sibling was breathtaking.

There are some behaviors and attitudes that our children exhibit that seem to come from outer space, because they are alien to our own thinking. I remember the time I asked our oldest son (then about six) if he would weed a patch of my flower garden for 50¢ an hour, and he agreed. About half an hour later, I noticed that he was in the family room watching TV. I said I thought we had an agreement, and he said, "Yes, and I'm paying Scott (then three) 25¢ an hour to do it." I couldn't believe I had raised such a "capitalist" and slave-labor boss! As I lamented to a friend about young Billy's apparent lack of desire to be a joyful worker, she put things into perspective for me: "Arlene, some people are just born leaders and have the skills to oversee others. Maybe he will grow up to hold a position of authority." (P.S. He is presently a Captain in the Air Force, working toward the rank of Major. And all I ever got to be was a major-*ette*!)

Years later that same son came in and asked, "Mom, are we poor?" (I usually try to get to the root of the question before answering, so I'm not off on a tangent like the little boy who asked his parents where he came from and got a thirty minute facts-of-life lecture, and responded, "Oh. My friend Joey came from Pennsylvania."). I asked, "What makes you think we're poor?" He replied, "Because Tommy across the street said we are." Hmmm, I wondered, "And why does he think that?" Billy replied, "Well, his family gets a new car every two years, and we have old cars."

That opened the door to a discussion that each person has a certain amount of resources, and that decisions must be made about how those resources can be used in different ways. "For example," I explained, "instead of new cars, Dad and I have chosen to provide camping vacations for you children each year so you can see what a beautiful and wondrous land the Lord created. Also, we use some of our resources in supporting the hunger program, missionaries and other charitable works. Would you rather we had new cars?" His eyes grew wide and I could tell he had "bought into the program" when he replied, "Oh, no. I like the way we're spending *our* money."

We bought a Weimeraner puppy when the children were young, and five-year old Scott remarked at how big his paws were, and how much "loose skin" he had. I explained that the paws were evidence of how big he was going to grow, and the loose skin was because he hadn't grown into it yet. Weeks later when Scott was giving me a shoulder massage, he remarked, "Mom, I can tell Dad's a lot older than you." I asked how he could tell. He responded, "Because he's so much bigger than you! But you're going to get bigger when you finish growing up. You've got lots of loose skin up here!"

Going back to economics again, Scott, came to me one day and asked, "Can we have an Intellevision?" (Intellevision in the 1970's was the forerunner to modern-day computer games). I told him no. The next day he asked, "Mom, when you said we couldn't have an Intellevision, did you mean: #1, that you wouldn't spend your money on it, or #2, that you wouldn't allow it in our house even if you didn't have to pay for it?" (Wise young man even at age ten, eh? Always checking things out!)

I replied that, "As to #1, it is true that I wouldn't spend my money on it, and as to #2, I wonder how a $200 item would find its way into our house without someone knocking on the door and asking to speak to me." He said, "No, I mean if Christy and I earn the money ourselves to pay for it, would you let us buy one?"

I counted myself as a pretty "savvy" Mom who never said no when I believed that natural consequences would rule things out in time, so I said, "Okay, if you can earn the money yourselves, you can buy one." (Where and how were a ten-year old and an eleven-year old going to raise $200 in the days when we were paying 50¢ an hour for babysitters?)

A couple of days later they came home all excited, with $12 in their little hands. They had hired themselves out around the neighborhood, had walked dogs, picked seeds from a thorny plant for the nursery, and washed cars. Scott said, "This may take more than a year!" They saw an ad in a magazine for ordering first-aid kits as a fund-raiser and asked if I'd advance the amount for a carton. I looked at the ad and said I didn't think people would pay $3.50 for the first-aid kits (which consisted of a dozen band-aids, some gauze, tape and antiseptic), but I was willing to advance the money on the condition that I would be repaid out of the first sales. Agreed.

When the kits arrived I was even more convinced that this was not a very viable item, but three weeks later all three dozen had been sold! They had made a profit of $60! Some time later they saw an ad for ordering gift-wrap and notepaper as a fund-raiser, but I was even more skeptical about that product which seemed to be of inferior quality at a high price. However, I agreed to the same deal on advancing them some funds to buy the carton of supplies. I was stunned when they sold the entire carton in six weeks.

By that time, the price of the Intellevision had dropped drastically and they were within about $10 of their goal. They had shown considerable fortitude and responsibility in sticking to their commitment, so Bill and I gave them the final amount they needed and they bought their long-awaited purchase. Ninety-eight days after they had bought it, the Intellevision stopped working. I took the children to a repair shop where they learned it would cost $58 to repair. Scott was upset. He went to the library to find out the name of the president of the company and wrote a lengthy letter asking, "Is the reason you give a 90-day warranty because you only expect your product to last a short time?" A few weeks later I got a call from a customer service representative asking about the letter. I said, "That was written by my son, and he's the one who knows the details; you'll have to speak with him when he gets home from school." She called back, spoke with Scott, and the bottom line was that he got a new Intellevision from the company. I saw a young man's determination, not to quit the race in the middle, lead to a successful outcome to his problem.

I should add that I observed an additional scenario unfolding as brother and sister went around the community with their fund-raising projects. Sometimes when Christy would come home after canvassing the neighborhood, she would say something like, "I met a sick, old lady who wanted the notecards but didn't have the money, so I gave her a box, free." Christy then had to make up the difference out of her allowance, since those cards were not hers alone to sell. Sometimes she would stop back at that person's house to visit and bring a little hand-written note of cheer. Occasionally she'd ask if we could spare a muffin or other homebaked treat for her to take, so the lady could have something with her tea. I was privileged to observe a heart being formed.

A few years later Christy decided that the people at the nursing home might enjoy some violin music, so she would strap her violin on her bike and head off to play for them. She even took the time to place the fingers of 80-year-old Abe on the strings and show him how to hold the bow. He said it was one of the thrills of his life, because he had always loved violins but never had held one before.

The Bible admonishes parents to raise up their children in the way they should go, and promises that when they are old they will not depart from it. I've watched wee tiny seeds of direction that I've planted turn into creative and caring deeds by my children. And now in my "gray years" (even though I've been Gray for over thirty years already), I am seeing that same sort of kindness and caring in my grandchildren, encouraged by *their* parents. The Lord is faithful from generation to generation, and His mercies endure forever!

I Stand at the Door and Knock
(or Ring the Doorbell)

My daughter had to have some growths removed from her back and asked me if I would take her younger child, two-year old Brandon, for about a week while she healed. I drove up to St. Petersburg, picked up Brandon, and we started back on our four hour trip to Ft. Lauderdale for the rainiest nine days in the city's history. Each day Brandon's limited vocabulary announced, "It wainin'." And each and every day it "wained!"

The day before I was supposed to drive him back home, my mother told me about a surprise 60th birthday party for a cousin. It was to be held at the home of the woman's daughter, who had two young children of her own. My mother thought it might be an opportunity for Brandon to socialize a bit, and the hostess said we'd be most welcome to attend.

I had remembered the birthday-lady once telling me that her grandson never paid much attention to her, but I thought that meant she just wasn't getting the amount of affection she desired. However, upon seeing three-year old Adam for the first time, I was acutely aware that there was a problem. He was totally oblivious to people arriving at the party, and seemed to be in his own little world. My mother told me that the supervisor of the daycare Adam and his sister attended had suggested that he be tested for autism. However, his family's reaction was that the supervisor wasn't a medical professional and had no training in these matters. They had taken the children out of the daycare and arranged for someone to come to their home to care for them. With this background in mind, I was most reluctant to broach the subject with the parents.

A couple of weeks after the party, I felt a very strong nudging to go to the parents and talk to them about autism. I reminded the Lord that they had already had the subject brought to their attention and had made it perfectly clear that they didn't want to hear any more about it. So that should close the matter. Right? Well, not exactly . . . When the Lord has a plan in mind, He doesn't abandon it easily. I argued, "Lord, how can I go tell them that You sent me? They know I am a Christian, and they are Jewish. So if You're going to insist on this, You're going to have to give me Scripture from the Old Testament to validate this for them! I know You are the One God of both Christians and Jews, but I'm going to need some confirmation that they can relate to, before I go and say 'I'm here at the bidding of the Lord'."

Even though the Lord provided an appropriate and suitable promise from the book of Jeremiah, still I procrastinated and tried to evade the mission. Nevertheless, the Lord's urgings did not abate. A few nights later, with fear and trepidation, I drove to the parents' house and rang the doorbell. It was evident that they were getting ready for bed, and were obviously surprised to see me. I mustered a weak smile and said, "Do you have a couple of minutes?"

Once inside, I pulled two library books out of a bag and said, "I'm here to bring you *hope*. I'm not a doctor, and I don't know whether or not Adam has autism, but if he does, it's treatable. These books are about two different boys whose families used very different methods, but both young men have made remarkable progress and are living productive lives now. And I believe Adam can do as well. I'm here at the urging of the Lord, and He gave me this reassurance for you from the Book of Jeremiah 17:7, "Blessed is the man who *trusts in the Lord*, whose *hope* in the Lord." and from 31:17 "There is *hope* for your future, says the Lord; your sons shall return to their own borders."

I asked them to read the books with hope, and then I got out of there as fast as I could, leaving behind two very bewildered people who hardly knew how to respond to my unexpected visit. When I got to my car I put my hands on the steering wheel and then laid my head on my hands and announced, "Okay, Lord, I did it. It's over!"

But it wasn't "over." In fact, it had just begun. Within a few weeks, they decided that the husband, who was a teacher, would quit his job to stay home to work intensively with their son. Less than three months after that, Adam---who had never comprehended what being "potty-trained" was all about---was dry and clean, day and night! Some weeks later he was saying simple words to indicate that he wanted something to drink. His word for juice was a slurred "juuuuu," but it sounded like music to his parents' ears. Merely two years have passed to date, and he continues to make progress step-by-step.

As for me, I am ecstatic! How could I have doubted the Lord? He has never led me astray, and He has never been unfaithful. So why do I continue to be hesitant when I feel Him calling me? 'Tis a puzzlement. But one thing about our God: He is wondrous, and he is **patient**. He allows me to follow at my own pace, gently nudging and encouraging me each step of the way, but allowing me time to come to the decisions myself.

I have told Adam's father that had I but guessed what lay ahead, I would have been more eager---no, I would have RUN *barefoot* to their house that night! It is nothing short of a miracle to see the Adam of today, versus the little boy so lost in his own un-reachable realm just a couple of years ago! And all because the Lord finally convinced a hesitant messenger to ring a doorbell and have a door open for Him to enter so He could bring His hope, His love, His healing touch.

Two, Four, Sex O'Clock, Rock

For several years I was a volunteer at an emergency pregnancy counseling center called "Birthright." My role was to encourage, support and reassure, and to bring some semblance of calm to the frightened young women I encountered.

One day I arrived a few minutes late, and felt a bit flustered as I fumbled with my keys to let two waiting girls in. I went to a private office with one of the girls, smiled gently at the nervous teenager and asked how I could be of service.

She told me her name was Cindy, and that she was sixteen years old. She said she had come for birth control pills. I was puzzled, because we did not dispense birth control but rather did pregnancy testing and support services for pregnant women. I asked her how she had come to seek out Birthright's help, and she said, "Isn't this a woman's clinic?" I said that it was, but the more we spoke, the more I realized she was at the wrong address. Unbeknownst to me prior to that day, there was another clinic at the far end of the shopping strip---one called "A Woman's Clinic," where abortions were performed.

When I realized the mix-up, I asked if she would like to talk for a few minutes anyway, and she seemed relieved to be able to do so. In answer to my inquiry as to why she was seeking birth control, she told me, "Well, nothing has happened yet, but I can tell it won't be much longer. My boyfriend says he can't live without it."

A strange series of questions began to form within me. I found myself asking her what she thought the percentage of sex in a marriage was. She said about fifty percent. I said, "You mean, twelve hours a day?" "No," she sheepishly replied, "it's probably ten percent." If that were so, I explained, it would require 2.4 hours a day. Once again she revised her estimate, this time to about five percent. I said, "Cindy, imagine you have two children involved in soccer, your husband has a meeting after supper, and you still have to manage 1.2 hours every day for sex. Do you think that is likely?"

I explained that while sex was an important part of marriage, it was just that: a *part* of marriage, and in order for marriage to be successful it had to be grounded on mutual respect and values, shared goals and responsibilities, reciprocal support and help, and a willingness often to put aside one's personal desires to be of service to one's mate. I said that in all our discussions about her boyfriend I hadn't heard her refer to his concern for her, only repeatedly that he couldn't live without "it."

"Cindy," I asked, "are you content to be someone's 'it'? What happens if you are incapacitated or sick? Is he out looking for 'it' with somebody else? And are you willing to be an 'it' for perhaps four to six boys between your sixteenth birthday and your twenty-first? A strong "No!" was her response, but I explained that once she got onto a sexual superhighway she would find herself at a destination where she did not want to be.

We spoke about the necessity of making decisions about one's life for oneself, rather than letting other people pressure us into things we did not believe were right for us. And we talked about how God had a plan for her life.

Suddenly she was crying. She got up, walked over to me and hugged me and said, "Nobody has ever talked to me like you just did." As she prepared to leave, I asked her if she was going to the other clinic to get birth control. "No," she replied, "I'm going to get another boyfriend!"

That morning, I had prayed that the Lord would use me, and as I allowed myself to be led by the Holy Spirit, I found that He had a far different agenda than I'd had in mind! As I reflected on the morning's events, I laughed out loud at the interesting questions about "percentages" that had formed on my lips. What a privilege to have been part of teaching His child, Cindy, about His great love for her and the great gift of love-making He had planned for her life!

Rock-A-Bye-Bye-Baby!

During my years of volunteer work at Birthright, I encountered many different situations, but none more challenging than the day I found myself in possession of a two-month old Navajo baby girl. The day started off normally enough, but in the course of my transporting a young mother and her baby for an interview for housing, we discovered that the housing did not include the baby. Uh, oh. What now? It was getting late in the day, and the mother said, "Please take the baby." I tried to protest that I didn't have any facilities for the baby at my house, and absolutely no way to transport her. She said she had a plastic bathtub and we could fill it with towels for cushioning.

Before I knew it, I was in the car with an infant in a bathtub, and wondering how I was going to explain this at home! I dug out the old bassinette and cleaned it up, and while I fixed supper I put the baby on a blanket on the living room floor where I could see her while I worked. (That location was also visible from the front door). It had been about twelve years since there had been a baby in our house, and I figured we'd have to make some hurried adjustments.

Soon I heard my husband's car pulling into the driveway, then the sound of the front door opening and closing, but when I looked down the hall there was no one there. I opened the door and there was a very confused Bill standing outside. He asked, "What in the world is going on, *now*?" I told him about the predicament the girl was in and assured him it would only be for a few days. "Come in," I said, "because you're going to have to babysit while I go to a meeting tonight." (Not perfect timing, eh?)

Serena was a good baby---*except* when the bottle was taken out of her mouth for a burp. Then she became wild, throwing a temper tantrum that would have made the Guiness Book of Records for two-month olds! She had never been held during a feeding; always the bottle had been propped up and she was allowed to drink without interruption---a full 8-ounces at a time, in fact! She arrived at our home accustomed to drinking FIVE 8-oz bottles a day; that's forty ounces of milk for a two-month old!

The first night she awoke for a 2:00 a.m. feeding, but the next day after I realized how much she was inhaling, I decided to take her off that fifth bottle. So on the second night, I simply did not provide the feeding. On the third night she whimpered pitifully, as though to say, "I'm never gonna get a bottle from Hard-hearted Hannah!" (By the third night she was sleeping through the night.)

When she had been with us for a few days, we were all getting used to having her around, and beginning to enjoy her, too. One night my parents came for dinner and towards the end of the meal I noticed that 15-year-old Billy had finished eating just at the moment Serena was beginning to get fussy. I asked him if he'd see to her while we finished our meal, and he went into the next room with her and her bottle. I could hear him talking softly to her, and she settled down and got quiet.. After I cleared the table and got the dessert dishes out, Billy came back into the dining room holding a sleeping baby, who looked like a little angel, in his arms. My dad looked up at our gangly teenaged son cradling the baby and said, "Look's like Billy's learning to be a daddy." My eyes stung with tears as I realized that my own "babe" was growing up so fast. So soon, Lord. And as I saw how gentle and tender he was with this little bundle, I realized that he had qualities deep within that he rarely let others see.

Through a turn of events, Serena was part of our household for a full month, and when it was time to "return" her, I knew that we had all grown very fond of her and that it would be difficult to say goodbye. I thought of all the foster parents who have to do that regularly, and I prayed that the Lord would give me the strength of character to be gracious under pressure. She was--and is--*His*, after all, and He just let us share in one of His most perfect works for a short while.

I remember hearing that "Babies are evidence God hasn't given up on the human race." I still think of Serena and pray that she knows that God holds her in the palm of His hand.

As Far as the East is From the West,
Are My Thoughts From Yours

I think I know how Joshua and most of the prophets must have felt. There have been times when I have felt a nudge to do something that seems so outlandish that I am *sure* the Lord has dialed the wrong number! I know I am not "qualified" to do what He asks me to do and I argue with Him that I am not able.

But after all is said and done, and I reluctantly go where He sends me or do what He asks of me, I am blessed to see what He can do with a simple willing vessel. And that is, after all, what I am. I have no extraordinary talents, no special abilities, no particular gifts. Probably the only attribute I do have is a fairly receptive spirit (even though I do debate the issue before yielding completely).

Once, while I was working at Birthright, there was a young pregnant girl who said she had nowhere to live. She said her mother had "kicked her out," and she had nowhere to go. From our discussions, I knew her mother would not be receptive to a visit from me, and I asked the Lord to somehow "fix the situation." That night when I went to bed I had a vision: I recognized myself in the vision, but I was astounded at how almost ethereal I appeared. Jesus was standing opposite me with His hands on my shoulders, and I knew that meant He was sending me forth to go to the girl's mother. I adamantly requested that He find someone else, but I knew that the decision to send me had already been made. I suddenly noticed that although I sensed His hands on my shoulders, in actuality the sleeves of His robe were empty. He said simply, "Go and reach out your hands in My place." What does that *mean?*

A few days went by and I still had not gone to see the woman. I was hoping for a reprieve. As I worked in the garden one afternoon, Bill came home unexpectedly early from work and Scott said, "Dad! You're home early. Maybe we can get a pizza so Mom doesn't have to cook since we're dirty from weeding. Then afterward can you take me to get some camping equipment for Boy Scouts?" Suddenly I was relieved of having to cook dinner---and "coincidentally" the place my son needed to go was down the road from where the woman lived. (Are you making a way, Lord?) We were soon on our way to our respective destinations--Scott anxious to go shopping, and me dreading the encounter that lay ahead.

I rang the doorbell and when the woman opened the door and found out who I was, she *nearly* closed the door in my face. Somehow she hesitated, and in that split second I asked if she had just a few minutes for me, since my husband would be coming back to pick me up after he ran an errand with my son. Perhaps she felt more secure knowing that the visit would be short, and she let me in.

I had hardly begun my plea for her daughter, when she cut me off. Her daughter was an ongoing problem: drugs, truancy, lying, stealing, cheating--and the mother was not about to take her back! I listened to a litany of complaints and realized there was no easy finale to this scene. I tried a new tack: "But she's your only daughter," I started to plead. "No! She's not! I had a baby girl twenty-five years ago when I was 18-years-old, and gave her up for adoption!" She started to cry, and she told me she had done it on her own and had never even let her own mother know what she was going through.

As she poured out her story, I walked over to the couch where she was sitting. I sat down next to her and put my arms around her. I suddenly felt as though I could see *through* her body and clearly "saw" my hands behind her back. I remembered: "Go and reach out your hands in My place." While I had *thought* I was going in behalf of the daughter, *I was actually there for her mother instead!*

Just as Joshua had no idea that the walls of Jericho would come tumbling down, neither did I know that the Lord wanted to pull down some old walls in that woman's life. He allowed me to watch as He reached out His hands in her life, using my human hands as His instrument! Lord, I pray that I will learn not to second-guess Your plans, and that I will be increasingly more willing to respond "Yes, Lord," when You call me to a challenge I do not comprehend.

62

"When You Saw Only One Set of Footprints, That is When I Carried You"

Our family housed young pregnant girls at different times as they awaited the birth of the babies they would bear and in turn give up for adoption. Before we embarked on this venture, we discussed the possibility with our children, and one of the questions was how we would work out sleeping arrangements since we didn't have a spare bedroom. Nine-year old Christy said, "I'll move in with Scott (eight) while she's here, because if she can give up nine months of her life to save a baby's life, at least I can give up my bedroom."

Our first guest arrived unexpectedly in the midst of some renovations we were having done on our house, and she learned how to search each day for the current location of the microwave, refrigerator, etc., which were constantly being moved as though they were part of some kind of moveable Scavenger Hunt! Monica had been brought to Ft. Lauderdale from another state by her mother, because the mother's Ob/Gyn had moved there and she wanted her daughter to be under his care. Monica had gone out with the father of the baby one time and the pregnancy was the result of date-rape. The plan was for her to have the baby and give it up for adoption.

Monica, however, had several "modern-thinking" siblings who regularly called long-distance to convince her to have an abortion. I uncovered a secret plot to "kidnap" her from our house and take her for an abortion, so she could "get on with her life." I told her I wasn't going to police her activities and that she was going to have to be responsible for her actions; but I did ask her to consider that there are no two people on the earth exactly alike, and that her baby was a uniquely special creation. Monica said she could never have an abortion and waited out the pregnancy to give the baby up for adoption. But it was a difficult time.

My children hovered over Monica in a smothering way, and in an effort to get them to back off, she tried to make light of the situation. One day my son came in and said, "Monica said that being pregnant is no big deal. She wanted to have a baby someday anyway, and now she'll know what it is like." I responded, "Oh? Well, lay your arm up here on the counter and let me smash it with this hammer." "*What? Why*?!" I continued, "Well, someday you'll probably have a broken arm, and now you'll know what it is like." He looked incredulous, so I explained, "You see, Monica didn't really mean that being pregnant is no big deal, because *it is*. What she wanted to say is that she'd like you and the others to back off and give her a little space, okay?" The children got the point.

On the day of her delivery, I was at the hospital with Monica. Following the birth, her eyes shone brightly for the first time since I had met her over six months earlier, and the first words out of her mouth were, "You were right, Arlene. This *is* a very special child!" Monica spent about half an hour sitting in a rocking chair holding the baby, and I could see her through the window talking softly to the little one. When she came out of the room it seemed as though her feet didn't even touch the ground, and she was in awe at the wonderment of new life. She told me she had said goodby to the baby and that she would be all right now. And she was. About a year later she married a wonderful young man who admired her courage and stamina in dealing with the situation as she had, and they now have two precious children of their own. I have seen her grow and mature over the years and have thanked the Lord for His tender mercies in helping her embrace a mature decision when she was just a teenager.

A second girl, Vicky, really didn't want to give her baby up, but her family wasn't willing to take on the years of responsibility for child-rearing while the girl went back to college and got established in a career. Vicky's parents had raised six children of their own, and when Vicky announced she was leaving home to move to Florida to live with a young man, both of her parents had hugged her and told her they loved her, but they asked her not to start her life's journey in that manner. Then when Vicky got pregnant she expected them to change their lives and make her wrong decisions turn out right. Vicky and I had lonnnnng talks, but nothing I said made a dent in her thinking that *if only* her parents would raise the baby for a few years, everything would be all right.

I had arranged for Vicky to have a birthing coach with her during the delivery---a woman who was a nurse and who had the training necessary for being a real help to her. One night the phone rang and Vicky said she was at the hospital. I went over and together we waited for the coach to show up. Four hours of labor later, still no coach. When it was time to wheel Vicky into the delivery room, she looked up at me and implored, "Would you come with me, please?" I said, "Sure," in a confident manner, hoping to allay her fears, and in a few minutes I was covered in a scrub-green uniform and facemask.

Vicky trusted the doctor implicitly and she also trusted me. When he gave her an order she did just as she was told. Between times, I stroked her forehead and encouraged her to relax. And she was so relaxed she almost seemed to be peacefully asleep. I kept glancing at the overhead mirror to judge when to tell her to open her eyes and watch, but suddenly I heard a baby's cry and was shocked to discover that a robust little baby had been born while I was preoccupied with getting Vicky to relax! She was so relaxed that *both* of us had missed the birth!

The next day I told Vicky I had never been present during a birth before, and in fact, for all three of mine I was anesthesized. She was incredulous. "You didn't say that last night!" she said. I conceded that I had not, because I figured the last thing she needed to hear was that I didn't know how to be of any help to her. We laughed together and she admitted that the disclosure was well-timed.

I went to court with Vicky a couple of months later when she officially gave the baby up for adoption, and both of us cried. She had prayed that she would receive a picture of the baby and that he would not be an only child. About two years later, against all governmental rules and regulations, the case worker gave Vicky a photo of the baby's first birthday, and told her that his adoptive parents were in the midst of adopting a second child! How faithful is our God!

It took Vicky about three years to come full-circle to an understanding that she could not expect other people to pick up the broken pieces of life caused by her willful irresponsibility, or wave a magic wand to make everything turn out right. She forgave her parents and was fully reconciled with them, and she accepted responsibility for the situation as it was. It was a long journey from rebellious teenager to God-fearing, faith-filled young woman, and I got to see the transformation in all the various stages. And today in place of that misguided teen, there is a lovely woman with a beautiful countenance whose delight is in praising the Lord and extolling His grace and mercy!

Both of these young women experienced the truth of that beautiful story about "Footprints"-- that the Lord had carried them in His arms when they could not carry on by themselves! And in an act of unselfish love and commitment, they bore their babes to give to strangers, knowing that the Lord would carry their babes in His arms, too.

When a Door Closes, A Window Opens

Some of us are late-bloomers. We even go to college late in life. . .in our mid-40's, when most of our contemporaries' children are taking their own SATs. That's the way it was for me. Thanks to the help of my teenage children who helped get me through the "new math" and some of the science, I was able to attain a college degree.

Part-way through, however, my husband said the finances for my education were no longer available, and it appeared that my college days were over. I considered ways to raise the money needed and decided to put an ad on the college bulletin board advertising my services as a typist/consultant for older students seeking college credit for past life-skills. In the program I was in, if a student could document evidence of having mastered skills and education in the course of his work experience, volunteer services or extra-curricular activities, he could receive college credit toward a master's degree. I knew that I didn't want to actually "write" anyone's personal story, and my first criteria was that the student write his own and then submit it to me for editing.

This turned out to be perhaps the most exciting highlight of my entire college career! Without exception, each person who sought my services was convinced that his life story would not be worth any credit at all, but after consultation and editing, every single one of the people I worked with received anywhere from 30-60 credits. No small feat! And the best part of all was seeing their reactions as they read through the final form of their manuscripts describing their lives and accomplishments. Every single one of them wept. It was truly a most satisfying endeavor for me.

I remember well the man who came and cried through our first consultation session together. He had been an alcoholic many years earlier, had lived on the streets, had lost his wife and children, as well as jobs, and didn't believe that his life had any redeeming value—and surely was not worthy of college credit! I asked a lot of questions, including where he was in his life at the present time, and told him to go back and write down *everything* —the good, the bad and the ugly—that he could remember about the preceding 20 to 25 years. It was a most contrite man who delivered about eighteen pages of hand-written notes several days later; but when we talked about whether he had seen the hand of God intervening in his life throughout his struggles, bringing him to the place where he now was, he became rather reflective.   The day he came to pick up his completed manuscript was a real high---for both of us! He couldn't stop crying, but this time the tears were of gratitude and thanksgiving, and my tears were of great joy at seeing him restored to a knowledge of the great love of his heavenly Father.

An elderly nun was one of my clients. She was _sure_ her life story was not worth college credits, but she proceeded to tell me about herself. In answer to some probing questions, she told me that at age fifteen, as a young girl in Cuba, she wanted to become a nun and live her life in service to the Lord, but her father was adamantly against it. She plotted and planned. She saved a small amount of money and stashed a few clothes in a hiding place, and when she was sixteen she stepped aboard a plane for the U. S., not knowing if she would ever see her native country again. She came to a land where she knew no English and where the customs were very different from her own ...as a teenager, with all the uncertainties that accompany one's formative years Over the years (she had been a nun for 47 years when I met her), she had instituted some innovative programs for orphans and had worked with children in a number of different places. She had a sensitive heart and a caring spirit. And no, she never did return to her native country. When she read her story in finished form she wept unabashedly. She received 40 credits in recognition of the programs she had begun over the years---a testimony to a life lived in service, obedience and submission.

There were a half-dozen more stories like these, each unique and special in its own way. After all was said and done, I praised God for the opportunity to have been part of this segment of my fellow-students' explorations into their past, and the chance to see them embrace their lives as having been touched by His hand.

If my finances had not dried up, I probably would have been denied the incredible experience of seeing deeply into the hearts of some special people, and helping them to have a new vision of themselves from the viewpoint of God. Thank you, Lord, for opening a window when a door is closed. And thank you, too, for entrusting me with such a sensitive and intensely personal project. Even after all these years it continues to touch my heart!

Straw. . . . berries! Get Your Sweeeeeeeeet
Straw. . . . berries!

As an older student, I came home from a college math test and believed I had "aced" it. I was on a high, and I wanted to share my happiness and gratitude with my family (particularly the teenagers who had nursed me through the "new math.") I walked in the door and announced to Christy, "Put on your jeans; we're going strawberry picking. Tonight's supper is LOTS of strawberry shortcake--- and a little soup to balance it out!" We picked eight pounds of strawberries. I had thought I'd make strawberry jam out of some, but when I saw how large and beautiful and perfect they were, I knew *these* strawberries weren't meant for "mashing" so I shared them with some neighbors.

That night I watched a TV show about a successful New York City businessman who wanted to experience what it would be like to be homeless. He took a two-week leave from work, picked up some over-sized shabby clothes from a local secondhand store, and let his beard grow to stubble. He dirtied himself up, dressed in the old, torn clothes and then headed toward the office building where he had worked for many years.

He was astounded to discover that although he passed many people on the street with whom he had worked and socialized for years, no one seemed to recognize him. He said that although the loneliness and dangers of streetlife were debilitating, after a week on the streets what was most frightening was that he had become "invisible." He realized that if he had became ill and fallen down, most passersby would have assumed that he was "just drunk."

All night I was plagued with thoughts of the "homeless businessman," and his words about having become "invisible" haunted me.   I imagined how awful that would be. The next morning I called Mary, a friend from church, and told her about the bumper crop of strawberries in the fields. I asked if she would like to go strawberry picking with me. She said she would, and then I said, "And we could go downtown and give them away to the needy and homeless." Her reply was, "And *do what*?!"

We picked twenty-eight pounds of strawberries and packed them into sixty-five little baggies, along with a strip of paper I had photocopied that said, "These juicy sweet strawberries are a gift from your loving God and Father."

We parked the station wagon on a seedy sidestreet near downtown Miami on a clear, bright day, and we proceeded to distribute ruby-red strawberries to the passersby. A couple of back-packing Scandanavian fellows were among the first of our incredulous recipients, and then came two frail, elderly women who cautiously wanted to know how much the strawberries cost. When we told them they were free, they said, "Ohhhhhh . . . on the last block we were on, a man followed us and wanted us to give him money, then we came around the corner and . . . here you are!" It was heartwarming to see their suspicion turn into precious smiles.

A poorly dressed old man shuffled up to us and we handed him some strawberries. In answer to why they were free, we explained that the strawberries were too ripe to wait one more day on the vines, and that this was something that we felt led to do. He insisted that he wanted to contribute, but I suggested that if he wanted to do a good deed, he'd have to think of something else. He left in a huff, and in about ten minutes he came shuffling back down the street toward us. He threw five wrinkled $1.00 bills into the back of the station wagon and his attitude *dared* us to say anything!

I smiled when I realized that while we had only given straw-berries to people heading up the street at that point, there was a different person headed toward us with a strawberry in his hand. I knew one of the recipients had shared! Then I looked up at the building under construction across the street and could see at least four or five men walking atop the girders eating strawberries; we had given a bag to only one construction worker. Suddenly I noticed something that caused me to call out, "Quick, Mary, let's close up the back of the station wagon and move on!" She asked what the problem was, and I pointed to the group of construction workers coming for strawberries. "They can easily afford to buy their own; these are meant for those who rarely have such a treat."

After a couple of hours, we had distributed all the bags filled with succulent treasure. Heading back to our homes, we reflected on the responses we had received and thought about how true it was that it was more blessed to give than receive. Jesus said, "The poor you will always have with you. . .," but at times like these, it was so fulfilling to see the lives of the needy enriched with the bountiful and gracious riches from the storehouse of the Father! And for at least that day, they knew they were not "invisible"---at least not to their Father!

Juicy, Sweet Watermelon . . . and Angels

Because my husband's job was all-consuming, I realized that if our children were ever going to experience the wonders of this vast and beautiful country of ours, I would have to provide the arrangements. It didn't seem feasible to take off cross-country in a station wagon with three active, healthy children under 12 who would probably drive me (and one another) crazy before we hit the state line. However, if we had a self-contained motorhome, I might be able to manage the driving and they would have a few places to stretch out as we travelled.

We found a used motorhome in good condition and began thinking of all the places we could go. I suggested to my husband that it might be a good idea for the children and me to set out in advance, driving to Denver, where he could fly in and we'd meet him.

After months of planning the trip in detail, we set off on our first "adventure" (the children being 8, 9 and 11 at the time) with a sense of excitement and anticipation. Before leaving, we each got the full allotment of library books we were entitled to, and stocked the little compartments of the camper with puzzles, writing paper and board games. We were to pick up Bill at the airport about a week later, but enroute we would stop and visit some friends and renew acquaintances.

On the fourth day of what had been up until then a rather uneventful trip, I was getting directions from someone on the C.B. whose "handle" was Longnecker. (He asked me what my "handle" was and I said, "Butterfly." He wanted to know how I got that name, and I said, "If you promise not to tell, I'm really a Gypsy Moth in disguise!") He was in an 18-wheeler and was hauling watermelons--- 1,900 of them. He asked how many of us were in "that house-on-wheels," and I told him there were four. When it was time for him to leave the road we were on, he said, "If you want to pull off behind me, I'll give you and the kids a nice watermelon as a souvenir." Back in the '70's we weren't concerned about hijackings, abductions, thefts, etc., and I was thrilled to have a watermelon so fresh it hadn't gotten to market yet, to bring to my old roommate, Terri, in St. Louis. We got to meet Longnecker and he gave us a nice, ripe, round watermelon, which we put under the dining table for safekeeping.

About ten miles later we were stopped behind a Volkswagen at a traffic light. One of the children was at the dining table in back, and two were stretched out on the bed over the driver's seat. The light turned green and the Volkswagen went about eight feet. I went about ten feet, catapulting the VW like a billiard ball right through the intersection and across four lanes of traffic, while I remained under the traffic light. For just a millisecond everything went black. Then I saw blood falling down from the bed above me. My heart raced as I thought I may have killed the children. Suddenly a drop hit me in the mouth and it tasted like the sweetest "blood" I could imagine! As my senses returned, I realized that at the impact the nice, ripe, round watermelon had travelled at about 20 mph to crash against the console next to me. It had exploded into millions of tiny pieces of flying debris and there were seeds *everywhere*! No one was injured, including the man in the VW, except that his car was in pretty bad shape.

I surveyed the damage to our motorhome and discovered that we had totalled the VW with the two bicycles we were carrying on the front, but there was no other *visible* damage to the motorhome. Unfortunately, there was some rather extensive internal damage. One of the bicycle pedals had punctured a hole in the grill and then went on to puncture the radiator, causing fluids to pour all over the street. When the policeman arrived, I was sweeping up the glass on the street, and he asked, "Are you all right?" With just one tear slowly rolling down my cheek, I meekly replied, "Yes sir."

I asked the driver of the VW why on earth he had stopped short, and he said that the light turned green and then immediately back to red. Several people at the adjacent gas station corroborated that the light had been malfunctioning all day, and the policeman

76

didn't even give me a ticket. I called the local insurance agent and asked whether he was duty-bound to call my husband (the policy-holder) if I reported an accident, and after assuring me that he was not, I asked him to send a tow truck. He came over within ten minutes and took us back to his office, picking up lunch for the children at a local fast food place on the way. He said he had books and a TV for the children, and that I was not to worry---he'd arrange to get me back on the road again as quickly as possible.

Unfortunately, the mechanic wasn't as optimistic and said he wouldn't be able to get the job completed by the end of the day. He wanted me to make arrangements to find a motel, but I told him we would just trust that he could finish it. I had been praying inter-mittently throughout the ordeal, and I knew without the Lord's inter-cession we were sentenced to staying in the motorhome in the service station's back alley overnight. A couple of times throughout the afternoon, the mechanic reiterated his belief that the job couldn't be completed that day, but I held steadfastly to my trust that it could. At last, at 6:00 p.m., we were on our way again!

Once again behind the wheel, I suddenly felt all the tension of the day washing over me, and I was feeling very tired. I called for directions on my C.B. and was guided by a friendly voice. I told him about the accident and he said, "I'm going to stop for coffee in about ten minutes, and if you'd like, I'll buy you coffee and some soda for the kids." Recognizing how emotionally tired I was, I said we would get off at the next exit, too. He was a pleasant fellow (nearly young enough to be my son), and after a short break I was ready to resume the trip to St. Louis where Terri was waiting. The coffee helped "reawaken" me, since I still had about three more hours to travel.

As we went through the labryinth of overpasses and entrance/exit ramps approaching St. Louis, I once more called for directions on the C.B. This time it was "Toy Boy" in an 18-wheeler who answered and guided me. I learned that he had a son and grandchildren who lived near us in Florida, and that he was hauling underwear. He said he was going to be getting off the expressway but that I should just continue and make a couple more road changes, and then I'd be there. I asked him if it were posible for him to take an alternate route and let me follow him, because as it neared 10 p.m., I was feeling tired beyond safe-driving limits. He agreed to alter his route and I was able to follow him for another 15-20 minutes to my exit. I asked if he'd pull over and let me shake his hand and thank him in person, and when he opened the door of his truck cab, out jumped a little old man less than five feet tall, who looked like all heart to me! I was very appreciative of his going out of his way, and I told him I didn't think I would have made it without him.

Lord, thank you for those whom you put in our paths to guide us when we are lost or tired or emotionally spent. Sometimes those angels look a lot like 18-wheeler truck drivers!

How Do **You** Spell Relief?

The second chapter of the ongoing saga of the watermelon scenario involved how we were going to break the news--gently--to Bill. After all, he was worried about my going off in the motorhome as the sole driver to begin with; how was he going to take the news that I had totalled a VW on my maiden voyage?

I swore the children to secrecy until I could tell Bill in person, preferably in a public place where he couldn't overreact too much. But there was the problem of the two bicycles that I had to discard. Wouldn't Bill notice that the bicycles were missing when we picked him up at the airport in Denver? How would I explain *that?*

My friend Terri said her children had two old bikes that she was going to give to the Salvation Army, and that I was welcome to take them. I rationalized (and hoped) that Bill probably wouldn't notice, so when it was time to leave St.. Louis, her old bikes were secured to the front bumper. (Shakespeare was right when he said, "Ah, what tangled webs we weave, when first we practice to deceive!")

We pulled up to the arrival area at Denver airport, and almost the first words out of Bill's mouth (after "Hello") were: "Whose bikes are those?" I was dumbfounded; Bill is not usually that observant. I tried to talk my way out of it in an evasive way, without actually lying. "They're the kids' bikes. How was your flight?" I asked. He responded, "Fine. But I don't remember a green bike." Me: "Well, it was always green. How was the food on the flight, are you hungry?" Him: "I'm kinda hungry. But I thought Christy got a *pink* bicycle for Christmas." Me: "Oh, did you?" (weak smile)

By this time we were approaching a restaurant and as I pulled into the parking lot I could see the children out of the corner of my eye; they were convulsing with stifled giggles. I flashed my "Be still!" look at them and parked the camper. As we got out and approached the restaurant, Bill once again reiterated his disbelief that the green bike was one of ours. I realized the jig was up, so I said, "You're right. It isn't. Terri gave it to me because I wrecked Christy's pink bike.

"How did you do *that*?" he asked. "Well," I replied, "I sort of did the same thing you did a few months ago to my bike that was on the rear of the station wagon. (He had backed up into a light pole and crushed my bike.) "Oh," he said. "And what did you hit?" We continued to walk toward the restaurant and were nearly safely inside as I mumbled, "A volkswagen ..." Bill asked, "What did you say?"

Well, it was all over. I told him that I had hit a VW but that only our bikes had been demolished. "What happened to the Volkswagen?" "Uh, it was totalled." He said that since I had hit the other car, our insurance would skyrocket, but I reminded him that I didn't get a ticket, we were all safe and sound, and that he might want to count his blessings. (P. S. Our insurance never did go up!)

Who Answers *Your* C.B. Calls?

During one of our motorhome jaunts out west, we were headed up through Flaming Gorge in Wyoming after a stop at Dinosaur National Monument. It was a beautiful day, though quite hot (about 106°) and our air-conditioner was really having to work. At the top of the mountain, just as we started our descent, I discovered that the brakes were not functioning properly. I shifted into low gear and gently pumped the pedal, but it became apparent that we were rapidly losing braking power. I turned the a/c off to try to conserve energy, but in a few moments the unmistakable smell of burning rubber began to permeate the motorhome.

I called to the children to gather all the sleeping bags and pillows as quickly as they could and place them around themselves and buckle up in the back. Then I called on the C.B.: "Breaker One-Nine, Mayday! Mayday!" (I didn't know what to say in an emergency, and Mayday seemed as good an appeal as any).

As though he had been waiting for my call, a response came back immediately: "Breaker One-Nine, this is the heavy equipment operator for the National Guard, what's the problem?" (*"Guard"*? It sounded like "God" to me!) I told him of our predicament and he asked our location. I said, "I am headed north and over my right shoulder I just got the first glimpse of the river at the base of the Gorge." He replied, "I know just where you are. And I believe the problem is that your brake fluid is overheated. You'll be coming to a level area shortly, and you'll be able to pull off and let the fluid cool down for about an hour. You should be all right after that."

Sure enough, about a mile down the road there was a rather level area beside a little stream, with some trees for shade. We parked the motorhome, got out some cold drinks and waited it out under the trees. After a "cooling off" period---(and don't we all need occasional "time-outs" in our busy lives?)---we were able to continue our journey, and our brakes were just fine!

I reflected on the words that had come back over the C.B. in my time of desperation: "I know just where you are." Doesn't the Lord say He knows everything about us, including the number of hairs on our head, and that He holds us in the palm of His hand? And doesn't He tell us that when we call, He will answer? (Hmmm, what a coincidence--------NOT!)

What's YOUR Destination?

(Three Tales in One:
Dance/Clowns - Pain/Healing - Need/Provision)

Many years ago I was part of a group of sacred dancers at church. We did not so much dance, as dramatize various Scripture messages or songs.

There was a 4-day Sacred Dance conference outside Boston one year and I was very happy to be able to attend with my group. One of the fun exercises we did was to dress up as clowns and go into the little neighboring village and discover that as clowns our freedom was boundless. Once in whiteface paint, we could no longer speak---at least not with words. But sign language and facial expressions were unlimited, and it was a real education to discover that people will accept the most outrageous behavior from a clown that they would never allow from a "civilian." I mean, where else could you step out in the middle of a street, put your hand up to indicate that traffic was to stop, blow an imaginary whistle, and have the driver <u>not only stop</u> but *smile* at you?

There were 120 of us, and that little town got inundated with clowns that day! Since we arrived by twos, threes and fours, each time one of our cars pulled up and the clown-passengers emerged, the surprised residents of the town would comment, "Oh, look--there's some clowns. . . . . And there's some more. . . ! Uh . . . There's a LOT of clowns in town today!" One man who was unable to get us to speak thought we were from the school for the *deaf*!

We distributed invitations to a church service to be held the next day at the college where we were staying. We didn't know if any of the townspeople would come, but were pleased to discover that many did.

I had a private agenda during the conference. Each day I had been prayerfully seeking some direction from the Lord regarding a trip in the motorhome that was scheduled to leave three days after I was to get back home. My concern stemmed from the fact that we were in the middle of a gasoline shortage, and each time I called home my husband told me that the situation was grim and that he didn't think I'd be able to start the trip. I knew that tempers had flared and that fighting at the pumps had broken out on a couple of occasions, and I didn't want to get stranded or put my children's safety in jeopardy. I asked for some sort of sign. "Lord, if I can't go, that's all right; just let me know."

On the last day of the conference, during an early morning praise session on the beach, I once again prayed, but this time I *demanded* an answer. With eyes closed and deep in prayer, for the first and only time in my life I heard the *audible* voice of God. It was so awesome---bold and resonant and full-bodied---that I opened my eyes to see if any of the others had heard it, but they all had their eyes closed and seemed unaware, so I closed my eyes again and gave my full attention to the Lord.

He called me by two terms, "Dear child," and "Silly girl," and the vision I saw as He spoke was of a woman standing with her back to me, one hand pulling aside a criss-cross curtain as she looked outside where a little toddler in a snowsuit was playing below the window. The Lord said, "Do you not know that just as the child knows not that his mother watches over him, so I watch over you always!" I was ecstatic. I was exuberant. I was humbled and yet lifted up at the same time.

On the way back to Florida I stopped off in New York to visit Aunt Jean, a favorite aunt who had been quite ill. At the airport someone came running through and stomped on my instep (doubly painful because I was wearing high heels at the time). The pain was severe and all during the flight to New York I was in agony. As I was getting off the plane, a woman noticed the button I was wearing that said, "Dance is Prayer Made Visible" and commented on it. We conversed as we walked to the baggage area and she commented, "The Holy Spirit is sooooo evident in you!" I laughingly replied,

"Well, I am in such pain right now, that it must be the Holy Spirit you are seeing, because my human face would be contorted with pain!"

When I arrived at my aunt's house, my relatives insisted that I needed to go to the emergency room, because it was evident from the swelling that I had broken a bone in my foot. I said if it was still swollen in the morning I would go to the hospital, but I didn't want to take my visiting time away from my aunt. That night I lay awake in excruciating pain nearly all night. The last time I saw the clock it was 5:20 a.m. I must have fallen asleep shortly after that, and at 8:00 a.m. I awoke and felt fully rested and the swelling on my foot was completely gone!

I flew back home that evening. My husband said I wouldn't be able to go on the motorhome trip, but I told him about my vision and the words of the Lord. Bill said that I should call AAA and tell them the route I had planned to use. I called them and they said there was no way I would be able to get the gas I needed. Bill said, "So you're not going, right?" "No, I *am* going," I replied. "But AAA said you couldn't make it," he argued. "Ah, but I have it on Higher Authority!" I replied with a smile.

Three days later the children and I set off for Buffalo, NY, where we were scheduled to pick Bill up at the airport for a vacation through Canada and Nova Scotia. We drove all day long that first day and noticed numerous signs along the interstate advising that there was no gasoline available.

By late afternoon, we were dangerously low on fuel and didn't have enough to get to our campsite destination. I headed off a ramp and reminded the Lord that He had said He watches over me and I had interpreted that to mean that He would provide gas. I rolled into a closed gas station and noticed a girl sitting on the curb next to the pumps. I asked if anyone else was around and she said, "The man is in the bathroom." When he came out I told him I needed some gas to get to a campsite, and I wondered if he had any for me. Without saying a word, he unlocked a pump. I asked him how much gas I could get (expecting him to say five gallons, which was the usual ration alloted during the shortage), and he said, "Get what you need." I told him I was on empty and the tank held forty gallons. He repeated, "Get whatever you *need*." I filled up! A number of cars formed a line behind me, but the manager told them he was closed!

Several days later, on the night before the 4th of July, I told the children that the gas stations would probably be closed on the holiday, and we were just going to have to bite the bullet and wait in one of the endless lines that were nearly two blocks long. Then I noticed one gas pump where there was no one waiting. I hesitated, then pulled up to it and sat in the motorhome for a minute, wondering if anyone was going to tell me to get in line like everyone else. But no one did! I pumped about thirty gallons and started thinking maybe it was another of the Lord's provisions and that perhaps no one else could even see that "phantom pump" and maybe no one would even come out and ask for payment! (On that last note I was mistaken, because someone *did* come to collect our money!)

When we got to Canada, for some reason there was no fuel shortage there, and in fact the gas prices were much lower than in the U.S., an added bonus for having planned a trip there during that time! Throughout the entire journey, whenever we needed gas, we were able to get it, and on more than one occasion we heard the familiar words, "Get what you need." The Lord sees to our needs and holds us in the palm of His hand through situations that seem impossible. And He's better than AAA in planning journeys!

Give Us This Day Our Daily Bread

In the early-1980's, Bill and I were invited to join about six other couples in Ft. Lauderdale to hear about a new concept in salvaging edible food for distribution to the needy. A man from Arizona had discovered that our nation's landfills were overflowing with food which was being dumped--*simply because it was surplus or marginally below quality-control and therefore unsaleable.* He said that in our area we could salvage over a million pounds of food a year for hungry people if our group would work together. The group which had been invited to attend represented different facets of expertise, including a wholesale food distributor, an accountant, an attorney (Bill--who could write the legislation needed to enable food-banking to get started in our State), an airline pilot (who could fly around the country making contacts with businesses), a man in the trucking industry, etc.

I remember thinking that a million pounds sounded like a pipe-dream, and I didn't think there was anything anywhere near approaching that figure of discarded food in South Florida. Fortunately, however, others in the group caught the "vision" that the man expounded, and within just a few months the workings were in order to open the first food bank in South Florida. At first, my only involvement was to have my suggestion for a name chosen. The new venture would be called "Daily Bread Food Bank," based on the Lord's supply of each man's need for daily sustenance.

A Food Bank operates like this:

♦ Companies with surplus food make it available to a Food Bank for distribution to charitable, non-profit organizations that feed needy people, i.e., the Food Bank would receive a phone call that a trailer truckload of food was available. (It might be baked beans that were mislabeled, orange juice that was a bit "off" in color," or, unbelievably, once because there were *double* the amount of raisins in a cereal! Customers buying the cereal the next time would have inundated the company with complaints about the "cutback," so the company simply removed it from the market.)

♦ The Food Bank would arrange for transportation to its warehouse. The agencies would make an appointment to come to the warehouse and choose from among the products available.

♦ Since the Food Bank didn't sell its products, it had to raise funding to cover the cost of the warehouse, utilities, trucks, fuel, insurance and staff. This came partly from a minimal donation by the agencies, but the majority was raised through donations and grants. Fund-raising was an ongoing and enormous undertaking.

After the Food Bank had been in existence for a couple of years, I got an urgent call from the director. He was in need of someone to work for him---immediately! He needed someone to do publicity, fund-raising, oversee the large volunteer program, and do a monthly newsletter. I was already stretched thin with several previously committed projects, including college courses, and I told him I lacked the expertise in the area of need he was seeking. He said he knew I had a "heart" for the poor, and that was more important than skills. I wasn't sure I believed that, but he was in a bind, and I reluctantly agreed to help out until he could find a more qualified person.

The 18 months I was at the Food Bank was the most physically and emotionally draining time of my life, and I was *always* over my head in deep water! I was treading water to stay alive and hoping I wasn't bringing the Food Bank down with me! I came to work in the middle of a huge fund-raising campaign called "Skip-A-Meal/Feed Another," which involved a mammoth publicity campaign, mailings to hundreds of churches and synagogues in a three-county area, coordination of press releases and television spots with all the major media, and a zillion other details that I've put out of my mind in order to maintain my sanity.

There was a small area at the Food Bank that we set up as a chapel, and I went running there regularly for guidance and support. The Skip-A-Meal campaign went surprisingly well, but there was no time to rest on one's laurels, because there were always several projects happening simultaneously in order to keep the operations afloat.

We did a canned goods collection at the Orange Bowl during a fooball game, a "Taste of the Nation" where two dozen of the top chefs came together and donated their skills at a fund-raiser, (delicious, but nerve-wracking to plan), and---with the help of a civic-minded TV news anchor---a professional video explaining the workings of the Food Bank (for which my job was to write the script. In order to emphasize the enormity of the waste problem, my idea for the opening was a bulldozer pushing a mountain of tomatoes toward the camerman. At one point I wondered if our insurance covered the cameraman if he got buried!). Nobody ever asked me if I had ever done any of these things before. And frankly, nobody cared. There was a job to be done, and somehow I was in it.

At one point we moved to a larger warehouse and there was a Grand Opening and Dedication Ceremony to be planned. Invitations went out to the mayor and other officials, leaders in the religious community, the agencies we served, members of the various companies that had donated food and services, and all the media. Most of those who had been invited said they would attend or send a representative, as the Food Bank had by that time become a well-respected entity in South Florida. I was instructed to prepare an agenda and invite certain people to speak. The Archbishop would represent the Catholic Church, the president of the rabbinical society would speak, and a pastor of a large interdenominational church would represent the Protestant churches. After we received word as to who would attend, my boss asked me, "Have you written the speech for the Archbishop yet?" *Have I WHAT?!* "Well," he continued, "it would be a courtesy for you to prepare a speech for him, and you should call his office and see if they want you to do it."

Throughout this story, I've tried to give an accurate picture of the "job" in which I found myself. At that time I was in my 40's and was nothing more than a high-school graduate enrolled in college for the first time, with absolutely no credentials for that type of position. Nevertheless, through the grace of God, this book you are reading was written by *a speechwriter to an Archbishop*!

One of the most memorable moments of my tenure at Daily Bread occurred during the distribution of Thanksgiving baskets. We distributed enough food to the 250 agencies to provide food baskets to over ten thousand people in a five county area, but there were about two hundred people who were not able to be involved in the agencies' programs. These had to be delivered one-on-one, and the Food Bank undertook that project. A couple of dozen volunteers, with cars overflowing with food, set out across the community. A man had called and said, "I'm an attorney and I don't want to just write out a check this year. Can you use me in some way to actually distribute food? I'll rent a truck or do anything you want." That was my first introduction to Arnie. He arrived early on the morning before Thanksgiving, and he and I were paired up to distribute food together. We went in my station wagon and I drove, because I was more familiar with the neighborhoods where the needy lived.

As we travelled along, I told him about the Food Bank and the various reasons people were in need. At one point he said to me, "You need to watch out; you're wearing your heart on your sleeve, and you'll get burned out!" Shortly thereafter we arrived at the apartment of an elderly little blind lady. She couldn't stop thanking and blessing us, and she reached for Arnie's hand and kissed it repeatedly. When we were outside her humble home, I looked over at Arnie and saw that he was filled with tears. "You'd better watch out, Arnie," I said, "You're wearing your heart on your sleeve, and you'll get burned out!" Arnie became one of the Food Bank's dedicated fund-raisers and was always available to do any task we needed. Part of the "perks" of the job was meeting all the wonderful volunteers I was privileged to work with.

And I was wrong to doubt the possibility of salvaging and redistributing a million pounds of food a year. A mere 16 years since its inception, Daily Bread Food Bank is distributing a million pounds of food *each month*! From day one, each Board meeting opened with prayer seeking the Lord's guidance and direction. And the Lord enabled the fields to be gleaned to provide a bountiful harvest for the needy. In Matthew 6:11, Jesus tells us to *ask the Father*, "Give us this day our daily bread". . . and I was privileged to play a small part in a group of believers who stepped out in faith and did just that.

"I Know the Plans I Have For You . . ."

One summer, in the midst of my college studies, we took a family vacation in the camper. After a couple of weeks of travelling around the Southeast we were headed back home to Ft. Lauderdale, and in another day or two our trip would be over. Late one night when everyone else was asleep (but I was awake), I had a vision that we were to go to a town in Georgia called Blairsville and start something to be called "God's Country." It was supposed to be "a place of healing and reconciliation". . . *whatever that meant!*

My usual mode of operating is to question and argue. I wish I could say that whenever I feel myself being led or directed by the Lord, that I simply obey quickly and quietly. Unfortunately, that it not how it is with me. Often I debate. I ultimately lose--but as a prelude, I stall.

In this case, I was confused about how He had seemed to open all the doors for me to go to college, and now THIS? Then I wanted to know, "*Where* is Blairsville?" Next, I whined, "And besides. I don't know anything about reconciliation and healing." "Ah," came the reply, "*but I do!*"

The next day I told Bill about the vision and, after looking at a map, bewailed that we were too far east to check out Blairsville on our planned route home. I tried to put it out of my mind after we got home, but to no avail. Every night the thought kept coming back like an obsession, encroaching on my attempts to sleep. Finally, Bill asked, "Do you think we should go up to Blairsville?" I told him I didn't know, but I did know that I wasn't sleeping because of it.

A few days later my mom came to stay with the children (then 11. 12 and 14), and we left early on the Saturday morning of a Labor Day weekend to fly to Atlanta and rent a car. Throughout the journey I was filled with doubts, and questions. We had to take a winding, narrow drive up over the mountain, and once we reached

Blairsville, there was little to tell us we had "arrived" . . . not even a single traffic light in the entire rural county! I implored the Lord, "Did you say *Blairsville?*"

We went to a real estate office to see various properties, but our guidelines were somewhat vague because we weren't sure what we were looking for. The salesman took us to a parcel of land and we walked several hundred feet to look at it. At the edge of a fast-running creek, I stepped on a yellow-jacket's nest and suddenly it looked like a scene out of an old "I Love Lucy" movie: We were racing back to the car through the field, arms flailing, trying to outrun hundreds of pursuing wasps determined not to let us get away.

Bill and the realtor were not stung, but I had numerous stings. Once in the car, the realtor headed to the hospital, because it appeared that I might need medical attention. And I was angry and arguing with God, "WHY did You make me get up at the crack of dawn, (I hate getting up early) to fly to Atlanta, to rent a car for that awful drive over that steep, narrow mountain road, to get stung and die way out here! Couldn't You have just "zapped" me in my own neighborhood?" But as I ranted---(and by the way, God can "take it")---I felt a calming peace wash over me. My heart which had been beating at about 500 beats a minute, suddenly felt quite calm and I told the realtor that a trip to the hospital would not be necessary. My stings, though painful, would not require medical care.

I started thinking that we probably weren't supposed to see that land, or maybe we weren't even supposed to be in Blairsville, but then I realized that if the enemy could discourage me and fill me with doubts, I would leave and scuttle the project. How could I let a Word from the God of the universe compare with a few pesky insects?!

We didn't find suitable property during that trip, nor on the next trip six months later, nor on two successive visits over the next year, but somehow because of the beauty of the area and the friendliness of the people, we still felt compelled to keep going back. Finally, about a year and a half after our search had begun, Bill and I went back without the children to spend a week looking in earnest. A friend from church mentioned that he had seen his "dream property" a few days earlier. We were excited for him and asked some questions about it. It was a 50-acre farm with a large 90-year old farmhouse, a big red barn, a one-acre stocked fishing pond, and it backed up to the national forest as an added bonus. The land was partly wooded, with gently rolling terrain, and three fenced pastures. But he said he wasn't going to buy it--it was just his "dream." We wondered if it might be suitable for us. He gave us directions and we considered going to see it, but we had a prearranged appointment with a realtor that afternoon. Somehow---("coincidence"?)---the realtor didn't show up and we couldn't reach him, so we drove out to see if we could find the farm.

It was a raw, drizzly day and the final blasts of autumn winds had blown nearly all the leaves off the trees, but we started off in the direction we had been pointed. After a series of turns we came to the property he had described. At the end of the long driveway, we found a widow packing her car with the last of her belongings to move in with her daughter about two hours away. She'd planned to lock the gate at the top of the road and would have been long gone if that realtor had kept his appointment! There wasn't a "For Sale" sign on the property, and once she'd locked the gate behind her, we wouldn't even have known the property was for sale.

Her name was Mae and she invited us in and offered us hot tea. It was cozy in the old farmhouse, and somehow we felt comfortable there, even though the furnishings were sparse since she was closing up the house and not planning to return. She insisted on walking with us over the entire 50 acres, pointing out good building sites, and getting us acquainted with the lay of the land. When we were leaving, we asked how we could see the property again after she left, and she said she'd leave gate closed but unlocked during the next few days that we'd be in town and she'd give her neighbor a key to the house if we wanted to see it again.

Each day we looked at different properties, and each evening we let ourselves in through the gate to sit on the old iron chairs at the pond, watching the sun set and the shadows grow long. By the end of our visit, we decided to call Mae at her daughter's and see if we could stop in to talk with her on our way back to Florida. This was a much more substantial property than we had anticipated getting-- (I had thought about eight to ten acres; this was over fifty.) We wondered if she would be willing to discuss some very unusual and creative financing. We came to an agreement on terms but said we couldn't make a final decision until we had spoken with our children and they had seen the property, because it was going to radically change our financial situation and they needed to be part of the decision-making. She said, "Give me a dollar to put in my Bible, and I'll hold the property until Spring-break when the children can come."

When we got to the car, I laughingly asked Bill if that is the way he conducted his law practice---a dollar for the Bible! (And if so, why was he late coming home for dinner so often?) We headed back to the Atlanta airport and stopped for something to eat on the way. I had been praying to the Lord for a sign to let me know if we were still within His plans or if I had gotten sidetracked---(I've have had that happen sometimes!) As we approached the restaurant there was a newspaper rack in front, and as I read the headline I got chillbumps all over. It said, in big bold letters: "GOOD TIME TO BUY NEW HOME." We bought a copy of the paper and I was grateful for the confirmation it provided.

Six months later when we closed on the property, both Bill and I stood with our mouths agape at the beauty of the property we had bought. We had worked out the terms in the bleakness of winter, and now in the springtime the land was alive with dogwood, apple- and blackberry-blossoms and wildflowers. It was breathtakingly beautiful!

There are additional stories which follow about God's Country Farm and how the Lord walked us through humanly impossible situations and how His Hand has been evident there in many circumstances. His ways are not our ways, and they are infinitely greater!

Unclench Your Fist and Turn Loose!

After the children and I had spent several summers sanding, scrubbing, painting, fixing and general renovations, and Bill had put up some cheery wallpaper that really transformed the old farmhouse, it was beginning to feel like "home." Then suddenly Bill announced that because of financial reasons we would have to sell the farm. I couldn't believe it. Once more---whiner that I am---I went to the Lord complaining about the injustice of it all. How could He let us work so hard just to have to sell it? It was so *unfair*! Then I remembered that God never promised us a rose garden, He just promised never to leave us! So I prayed that He would hold me through the gut-wrenching ordeal of parting with this beautiful mountain property so aptly called "God's Country."

About two weeks later, before we ever told anyone we were going to sell the property---not a realtor, not a neighbor, nobody---a car drove down the driveway one afternoon. I was working in the garden as the car stopped and a woman stepped out. She said she was from Albany, GA (about five hours away) and she explained that her daddy had lived here many years ago and had built the barn. Then she asked, "I wonder if you would be willing to sell the farm?" (IS THIS A TEST, LORD? Who ever drives down someone's driveway to ask if they wanted to sell their property?) A tear rolled down my cheek as I replied, "I wouldn't be 'willing' to sell it, but we might consider the possibility."

She was also filled with tears and told me that her daddy had died recently, and on his deathbed he asked her to promise to go back and buy the old homeplace. I called Bill in Florida that night and gave him the woman's phone number. He called her to work out the terms, and they agreed on a price that would bring a fair profit on the sale. Her mother and her aunt would be helping with the financing, so it wouldn't require an outside mortgage.

A few weeks later she made an appointment to come back with her mother, her aunt, and her daughter. I invited them to come for lunch. They seemed to enjoy their visit and were all excited about having the property back in the family again. As they were leaving, the woman said she was going straight to the lawyer's office and we'd hear from them later that afternoon or first thing in the morning.

They drove out the driveway and I never saw that woman again. I'll bet you're wondering why I never called her in Albany. Well, I never did want to sell it in the first place! And guess what. Bill never called her, either. Sometimes we have to nearly lose something before we really recognize its true value. And as for me, it's possible that I was too highly esteeming the farm, and the Lord tested me to see if I was willing to let it go, so that He could fill my empty hands with His grace. And when we got a second chance at keeping the property, it became even more precious to me--but only in its proper status of being subordinate to my relationship to Him!

Cooooool, Clear Wa-ter!

It was time to go forward with plans to open God's Country Farm to guests. If it was to be a place of "healing and reconciliation" as the Lord had indicated, there would have to be some comfortable accommodations where people would find rest and refreshment for their weary souls. We hoped to build three or four sturdy log cabins that would serve as a safe haven for our guests, but we were faced with the problem of providing water. Our old well at the farmhouse was pitifully inadequate, and we needed a new well to provide sufficient water for both the farmhouse and the cabins.

All of the well-drillers we spoke to wanted to charge us by the foot, but that was rather risky, since in the mountains you might go down anywhere from 150 to 500 feet before hitting a strong water source. One driller said he would do it on a flat-fee basis but that he would only guarantee water for the farmhouse. Once he had hit enough water for that he would stop, with no assurance that there would be enough for three or four cabins as well. We agreed to this and the drilling began.

I remember praying, "Lord, this was Your idea in the first place, and if You still want us to go forward with cabins, You're going to have to provide the water for them. And I don't want the driller to lose money on this either; his break-off point is 230 feet, and if he has to go beyond that he will be losing money on this arrangement."

The drilling began loudly and continued the entire day. From time to time I would ask how it was going, but there was not much sign of clean drinking water. About 3:00 p.m. I started to get a bit anxious. By 4:00 I was concerned. Around 5:00 there was apprehension in the air. They were already down to 200 feet, then 210, then 220. I started watching them measure: 225. . . 226. . . 227 . . 228 . . . and then the gusher, wildly spouting about a hundred feet up in the air! Pure, clean, clear water! (We had it tested--and it fits my less-than-scientific description perfectly). The driller looked incredulous and announced, "Welllll . . . you wanted water! You have enough water for the farmhouse and about a dozen cabins!"

Isn't that just like the Lord. He always provides more than we ask for. It's His way of saying "Watch and see what I **can** provide for you, oh ye of little faith!" It was such good water that my dad used to bring empty containers up to the farm when he visited and would fill up twenty or more gallons to take back to Florida with him. My heavenly Father provided sweet pure water for my earthly father to take home as a "souvenir."

But even more precious than the cool, clear water he provided, I am grateful that He is the Living Water in my life! He refreshes in a way that nothing else can!

Impossibilities?　No Problem!！！

On a bright Easter Monday morning--April 17, 1991--two 18-wheeler trucks each loaded with 82,000 pounds of building equipment pulled up at the top of our driveway.　It was an exciting moment!　Our log cabins were about to become a reality after months of planning, and the land was about to become God's Country Farm, a setting for visitors seeking a place of peace and tranquility.

One of the drivers looked at our long, narrow, winding driveway and the angle at which it travelled down the hill and announced, "We won't be able to get down that driveway.　It's too steep and too narrow for these big rigs."

"Really?　Well, what's the alternative?" I asked.

"We'll have to unload up here on the road and you'll have to get everything down by forklift." he replied.

I looked up at the "everything" he referred to and calculated that there was over 160,000 pounds of 24-foot long solid logs, roof trusses, doors, windows, etc.　Even *if* we used a forklift, the length of the logs would necessitate cutting down dozens of huge trees that lined the quarter-mile long driveway.　The only response I made aloud was, "hmmmm," as I turned aside and started praying feverishly!　One driver turned to the other and said, "I don't think she understands!"　Oh, but I did understand---*perfectly*.　And I knew that I needed to seek help from the only One I knew Who was able to figure out this dilemma!

After nearly an hour of figuring and calculating, a driver said he would try getting one of the rigs down the driveway.　At first he got the undercarriage hung up where the paved road met our gravel driveway, and for a little while he stayed hung up until they figured a way to get unstuck.　Then slowly, cautiously, he inched the big rig down that narrow pathway.　As it came to the first turn it looked like the top-heavy load was going to turn the whole truck over, but then it straightened out and made its way all the way down without a hitch. By this time a number of neighbors had come to watch the gyrations of the mighty rigs, and as the first one got down successfully there were cheers for the driver from the onlookers. (My own cheers were directed somewhat Higher Up!)

The foundations for the three cabins had been poured the week before, and now that the logs and all the supplies were delivered, the construction could begin. The huge logs would be cut to size on site. There was only one small hitch. We had booked a week's reservation for a family coming from Florida and I knew we'd be on an extremely tight schedule. I went to the Lord to "explain" the situation (as if the Lord of the universe needs little ole me to "explain" anything to Him!) But the facts were that the week of June 17th was the only vacation the family would have because the husband was a teacher who would be teaching summer school except for that one week; their son who had been in a detention center would be getting out and the family really needed this special time together; and sixty days was an awfully short time to get everything completed. The Lord's response was a terse, "*I know!*"

Not only did the construction have to be completed, but the furniture and furnishings had to be delivered and set up as well; carpet had to be installed; beds had to be made; the shower curtain had to be hung; kitchen cabinets had to be lined and dishes put away; curtains and blinds had to be up; and towels had to be hung on the towel rods, et cetera, et cetera, *et cetera*! But on the sixtieth day, when one cabin was *completely* ready for occupancy, I was absolutely filled with wonder--and awe--at the faithfulness of God.

It was amazing to watch such a substantial structure being erected with such ease. It reminded me of that verse in Scripture that says "Unless the Lord builds the house, the workers labor in vain." And for anyone contemplating a building project, let me recommend my "Foreman"-- He's "out of this world!"

Gliding Down the River, On a Lazy Afternoon

The weather was beautiful: bright, sunny and clear. A great day for an exciting tube ride down the river, now that the TVA was going to release millions of gallons of water from the dam. I was in my mid-50's, and I called my hiking partner, Tommy, who was in her early 70's, and coaxed her into going down the river with me. Tommy is a real "woman of the mountains," and won't take me on some of her more strenuous hikes because I can't keep up. That day she was hesitant because she had other plans; she had also injured her wrist a few days earlier and didn't have full use of one hand. Nevertheless, I persuaded her and we met near the embarkation point.

I really hate cold water, and I knew if I didn't jump in as quickly as possible, I might have second thoughts. As I jumped on my oversized truck tube and found myself in the midst of the fast-running river, I looked back at Tommy and called, "C'mon, chicken . . . what are you waiting for?" However, there are times when one needs to be more prudent, to think out a situation, to gather some information before acting. *This* was one of those moments. It would have been far better for me to have heeded that good advice, "Look Before You Leap." But-----too late!

I was floating backwards down the river and suddenly my tube hit something---one of the bridge supports. The force of striking it made my tube veer to the shore side of the support, rather than toward the middle of the river.

In an instant I saw that I was in danger. Lying across half the river was a huge fallen tree, with branches both above and beneath the water. I became entangled, and the strong current was beginning to suck me under, into the jumble of branches. I realized that if I were pulled under, I wouldn't be able to fight against that strong current to untangle myself.

As I grabbed for the branches above water, they broke off one after another, until I began to think my options had run out. By this time, Tommy was rapidly going downriver in the center of the stream and was unable to be of any help to me. She yelled for me to get out of the tube. I knew that *if*---(and it was a big IF at that point)---I were to survive, I would need that tube once I got untangled from the tree. At last, one of the branches I grabbed for held firm, and I was able to pull myself up and sit on a solid limb, holding onto my tube with my ankles. I hoisted the tube up and sat there for a couple of moments, panting and thinking about the mercy of God.

But I knew that *thinking* too long would have the same effect on me as pondering the coldness of the river, robbing me of what little determination I had left. I could picture myself becoming paralyzed with fear if I didn't act soon. So, putting the tube around my waist, I jumped back into the river and caught up with Tommy a hundred feet away where she had been able to steer toward some rocks to stop herself.

Although I was now much wetter (and colder) than I had planned to get on this tube ride (since I had been flat on my back with the back of my head in the water as I struggled to find a branch to pull up on), I experienced a most euphoric feeling of gratitude, thanksgiving and awe at the saving grace of God. It turned out to be one of the most awesome rides of my life, but I learned that it was important to focus on where I was headed and be aware of the signs and signals around me.

I asked Tommy why she had waited so long before jumping into the river, and she said, "I was checking out the situation. . . scouting out the places I might need to be aware of". . . (like that bridge support I ran into while going backwards!) It made me realize that God gave me a brain, eyes and ears. If I was so foolish as to not use my God-given talents, I could end up in disaster.

I was amazed that I could feel so exhilarated after such life-threatening circumstances, but then I reflected that it was God's grace filling me with a peace that passes all human understanding. So even though I had missed an opportunity to use my God-given abilities, He had come alongside and filled me with His strength and might . . . It gave new meaning to 2 Corinthians 12:9, "My grace is sufficient for you, for My power is made perfect in weakness."

What's In A Name?

Sometimes things seem like "coincidences," but when we look back studiously we see that there are far too many links to be mere chance. And I think the Lord sometimes gives us little "hints" to let us know that He has His hand in the situation, that we are right where we are supposed to be, and that all is well.

Here are some "coincidences" in my life that I believe the Lord used to reassure me during times of insecurity. The first time I gave birth to a child, my hospital roommate was named "Brown," and the delivery room nurse's name was "Green." Since I am "Gray," we had a rather colorful night that time! The second time I had a baby, my hospital roommate's name was "Brown." And the third time I had a baby, guess what? Yep, that roommate's name was also "Brown"!

When we bought our first house, our next-door neighbor's name was "Brown," and her mother's name was "Gray." We bought our farm from a woman named "Brown." I remember meeting a woman who told me her name was Brown, and I immediately hugged her and said, "Oh, you and I are going to be friends!" And we were.

I have learned to recognize "coincidences" as little lovenotes from my Father as He walks with me through the pathways of my life. Often when I seek reassurance from the Lord, He gives me a small sign to reassure me that I am "on track." I truly treasure these little gifts and appreciate the way He makes His presence manifest in my life. Some people would say, "My, what a coincidence." But I know my Shepherd, and He knows me . . . by name. (And He apparently knows all the Browns, too!)

Not by Might, Not by Power,
But by My Spirit Says the Lord!

It was summertime. I was at the farm waiting for Scott to arrive from college for the weekend. If he arrived before 5:00 p.m., we could just make it over the mountain to join a large group of cousins who were having a reunion at a restaurant in Helen, GA. By 4:55 p.m., I was getting anxious, but just then a familiar car pulled into the driveway and soon we were preparing to leave. For a reason I could not explain to Scott (or even to myself), I suggested that we bring a couple of items in case we decided to stay overnight, even though that was a very remote possibility. We gathered a change of clothes, toothbrushes, etc., and quickly started on what should have been a one-hour journey over the mountain.

We took Richard Russell Scenic Highway (a descriptive phrase for a beautiful but steep mountain road). We were making good time, and it seemed we'd make it. Suddenly, the motor quit, and I pulled to the side of the road. After trying to get it started, including an unsuccessful jump-start that a passerby offered us, we asked that a call be made to AAA.

We waited over an hour, and then came the big tow truck. The driver tried everything he could think of to get us going again, but said that it was an electrical problem and would have to be fixed at a service station. He said he'd take us back down to Blairsville, leave the car in the mechanic's lot and drive Scott and I back to the farm. No! I wanted to go to the reunion! It had been years since I'd seen some of those relatives and I didn't know when I'd get another chance!

I explained all this to the tow truck driver, and he sympathized, "Well, then I can take you over the mountain and leave you there if you think you can get a ride back." *I think I can, I think I can*, said the little red engine. Let's go!

At the first pay-phone at the bottom of the mountain, I called the restaurant (but by now we were over two hours late) and got a recording, "The restaurant is now closed; please call again tomorrow." I thought my cousins had all gone back to Sam's house, so I called there and got another recording machine. This was getting frustrating. "Sam, this is Arlene. My car broke down at the top of the mountain, but the tow-truck brought us down to your side, and I'm at the junction of . . .uh, . . . let me see what that sign says." (At the moment I turned to see what the number of the highway was, Sam's van came into view on the road leading from the restaurant. Still talking into the recording machine, I continued): "Scott, that's Sam's car! Run, Scott, run!" (Sam got such a chuckle out of that recording that he has preserved it for posterity.)

A cousin from out-of-state looked out the window of Sam's van and said, "Sam, there's a kid running behind us, waving his arms." And so we were "picked up." We stayed overnight at Sam's and the next day they drove us back over the mountain. We got a much longer and in-depth visit than just a mere dinner would have afforded, and the tow-truck driver got to see the hand of God provide a family visit when it seemed hopeless!

The next day when I pointed out to my cousins the spot where my car had broken down, I was amazed to discover that there were very few level places where I could have safely pulled off the road, and it was *exactly at the top of the mountain*. That was more than pure "luck"! Had it occurred a hundred feet earlier or later, I would have been left with no power brakes or power-steering on a steep incline, headed pell-mell down a sharp, winding road. Whew! Kinda took my breath away! I thanked and praised the Lord for His protection, His provision, and for the cooperative tow truck driver. I think that God---being our "Father"--- has a tender spot for *family* reunions, and granted me the desire of my heart so I could be part of that one. The power of the car engine failed us, but Our Father was there to pick up the slack. Thank you, Abba!

Blessed Are the Quilters
For They Shall Be Called Piecemakers

At a local summer-stock theater in North Carolina, just across the border from our farm, we attended a marvelous and moving musical production called "Quilters" several years ago. Little did I know then that it would radically change the course of my life. I saw it on a Friday before its scheduled Saturday night closing, and enjoyed it so much I decided to go back again the next evening.

Saturday morning, I went to tell my neighbor, Birdie, what a wonderful musical show it was, and I told her I was going back to see the final performance. I said, "Birdie, you would love it. I'm coming back for you tonight to take you to see it; you'd better be ready!" (Birdie is a widow in her 80's who rarely goes out, other than when a nephew takes her for an occasional doctor's visit). She protested that she couldn't go, but I insisted, "Birdie, you can wear that housedress, or you can change, but I *am* coming back for you tonight at 7 o'clock." (She was ready!)

I cried and laughed out loud both times I saw it, and Birdie laughed and cried, too. She said it was the most wonderful evening she'd had in nearly fifteen years. Birdie is a quilter, and I knew she would enjoy the production.

I had never done a single piece of quilting, but after that show I knew I had to do one in my lifetime. I asked Birdie to teach me. She asked what pattern I wanted to do, and without hesitation I said that I had always admired the Cathedral Window pattern. She told me that it wasn't really a beginner's pattern, but if I was determined and willing to persevere, she would teach it to me.

A few days later I was on my way to becoming a "quilter." She was right that the pattern wasn't a novice's project, but it was so fascinating that I was resolute about mastering it. After the basework for the pattern is done, it is a portable project that can be completed in small pieces at a time. At that point it is referred to as "lap-quilting," since it is done by hand and requires no batting, no backing, no frame, and no machine.

It wasn't long before I was working on my quilt every spare moment I could muster. It was beginning to take shape, and as the pattern unfolded I was mesmerized by its beauty. I carried it with me wherever I went: to waiting rooms, airports, ballgames, etc. It always attracted attention. People would ask what I was working on, and as I showed how the Cathedral Window pattern unfolded as the colorful "windows" were inserted into the base, they would invariably comment, "Oh, I see. Well, I could do *that!*" I would think to myself, "Yes, they could do the part they were watching me do, but it was the basework that was so tedious and time-consuming."

Over the next several months, my quilt attracted dozens of interested inquiries and I felt as though I was being prodded to make the basework available for sale. I vigorously resisted the notion however. The urge was coming from outside myself (or at least I should say it was not something I wanted to get involved in). I prayed to the Lord to see if this was coming from Him, and when He indicated that it was, I argued. Bill and I had just started the log cabin rentals at the farm, and I was about to become a grandmother, and I didn't think the Lord was taking into consideration that I could only be stretched so far! "Lord, I whined, "I know that one day is like a thousand to you, and a thousand like a single day, but have you noticed that I'm not a young chicken any more?!" His terse response was that "it will be good for Blairsville" . . . (at the time I thought, "whatever *that* means!") "And besides," I argued, "how do I know this is coming from You?!" "What's the name of the pattern, Arlene?" Awwwww, no fair, Lord! A cathedral window is a thing of beauty to give glory to God. It would have been easy to weasel out of if it had been drunkard's path, or deck of cards, or devil's ladder-----but cathedral window---something designed to give glory to God!

So in reluctant obedience, and still unsure of where this was leading, I prepared and packaged ten 12x12" squares of basework, which could be used for small projects such as wall-hangings, pillow-fronts, framed work, etc., and set off for Pappy's Marketplace. There I found a charming older couple who had a permanent booth where they sold finished quilts and crocheted pieces. I asked if they would allow me to set up a table at their booth to test-market whether the basework would appeal to purchasers. I said I'd give them 10% of whatever I sold. They agreed and before I knew it all the kits had been purchased. That seemed like a pretty good indication that there was interest in the basework. But I still didn't know where to go from there.

I named my new emerging enterprise "Cathedral Window Quilting SQUARES," and I started out by demonstrating at community centers, public libraries, recreational centers, and State parks. I envisioned that a "good year" would probably entail the sale of maybe 50 to 100 pieces of basework---truly a very part-time, sporadic enterprise.

Had I but imagined the exciting journey that lay ahead, I would have hastened to begin---nay, I would have raced! Even though I know that God tells us, "My ways are not your ways . . ." I never cease to be amazed at how very different His ways are! I walk in baby-steps; He strides across continents in a single bound. And His agenda is so far removed from mine. I have such narrow and shallow vision---He sees into the "heart" of the matter, because He is a heart-surgeon, and *that* is the realm in which He operates! I had thought this was about "quilting," but I was to discover that it was about people, and He simply needed an emissary to carry out His work. And as a side benefit, He blesses those who are obedient. The quilting enterprise grew and flourished; and in the process, so did I. And so did my understanding of how the Lord uses people to accomplish His purposes.

The Quilting Saga Unfolds,
Peace by Peace

After we close the Farm operations each Autumn, we return to South Florida for six months. My mother lives there, and it is where I was raised, so it is still home for me. The year I started the quilting enterprise, I heard that there was a quilt show near my Mom's, and that they had booths for rent where people could sell their work or products. With little expectation of what the scope of a "quilt show" was, I signed up for a booth.

There was a problem with my schedule, however. My friend Sharon's daughter was being married on the second day of the quilt show, and I wanted to attend. I arranged for a teenager to operate the booth for me for about two hours, which would enable me to dash over to the church for the ceremony about five miles away.

A few days before the quilt show, a friend from church, Cheri, came to see me because she was feeling disappointed that her husband wanted her to go back to work. He didn't seem to recognize that being a wife and mother to three school children was a job. I thought perhaps he was concerned about a college fund for the children and that perhaps a part-time job would satisfy the need. She said she hadn't considered that, but would check it out.

Since I was in the midst of getting ready for my first quilt show, I had quilting and display apparatus spread out all across my house. Cheri asked me what I was involved in, so I showed her the quilting and explained the process. She told me she had previously had a sewing business some years earlier and didn't want to get back into that. However, she said my project did seem interesting.

The day after Cheri's visit, the teen who was supposed to help me at the quilt show called to say she'd been invited to a birthday party and wouldn't be able to work. In the midst of my scheduling dilemma, I remembered that I had shown Cheri how the basework and the windows went together, and I called to ask if she could man the booth for me for a couple of hours that weekend. Fortunately, she was available, and both of us went to set up the booth. Cheri said she would stay for a couple of hours to get familiar with how the booth would operate, so she could do it on her own the next day.

Neither of us had any idea of how many attendees to expect at a quilt show, and we were astounded by the size of the crowd. It took both of us to operate the booth! By the end of the second day, it was apparent this was a viable enterprise. I asked Cheri if she would like to work with me, she accepted, and so far we've participated in over 50 quilt shows throughout Florida, Georgia and North Carolina, as well as Paducah, Kentucky and Houston, Texas, where attendance is nearly 50,000 people from all over the world.

My prayer before each show is that the Lord will not allow me to forget that this is His work. I ask that He keep me alert to those who are in need of His touch, and to use me for His purposes. Along the journey, I've seen the hand of God in numerous situations. There have been times when I've wondered, "Why am I here in Bartow, Lord?" (or Franklin, NC, or ???) and then I will encounter *one person* that the Lord wants to touch in a special way. I know it is not anything I am capable of in my own strength, and it never ceases to amaze me how the Lord will use me in an intimate way to reach into the life of a stranger.

Each situation is different---there have never been two alike. Once there was a girl who came to the booth with a small infant. I spoke briefly with her and cooed at the adorable baby. Later she came back at a time when there was a lull at the booth and I had time to spend with her. I looked at the mother, who was attractive and thought, she's only about sixteen or seventeen years old. The baby was happy and responsive to attention paid to her. I asked, "Is she about six weeks old?" The young mother said, "Yes, exactly." I continued, "And you're not much older than her, are you?" "No ma'am," she replied. How old was she? *"Thirteen,"* she confessed! I said, "You are a *wonderful* mother, and you know more about your baby than many much-older moms! She's a lucky little girl to be bathed in such love. You know, sometimes when adversity comes into our lives it is a time of real growth and a chance for us to seek and find the Lord in the situation." She replied that she knew that, and that the baby had changed her life. She told me she was being home-schooled and that she had a renewed commitment to persevere and succeed. It was obvious (particularly to me, after spending so many years at Birthright), that this was one of those rare success stories. She seemed to feel affirmation from a source far greater than my own mere human fountain flowing over her, as we spoke about the Lord's love for her and her baby. And after she was gone, I was left with a euphoric feeling that I had been allowed to extend His reassurance to this precious young lady!

Another time there was a woman who looked lovingly at the quilting on display, and then selected several kits to take home. As I stood behind her watching her make her choices, I placed my hand on her shoulder and something made me ask if there was a deeper significance about this particular pattern for her. She said it had been one her mother had done, and that day was the first anniversary of her death. I said I was glad she had come to my booth on that particular day, and as she worked on the kits, I hoped she would be flooded with wonderful, warm memories. There were tears in her eyes and she hugged me as she said she, too, was glad to be there that day. We both knew the quilting would have special meaning for her.

Once at a quilt show, a woman came up to me and told me her name. I recalled sending her a large order some years earlier. She had just gotten out of the hospital and heard an announcement about the quilt show on a local radio station. She said she was in pain, but had come in hopes I'd be there. That is the kind of comment that reinforces my belief that this is not merely a business, but a "ministry" as well. How many times do people buy a pair of shoes and think to themselves, "I hope I get to see the salesperson again"?

At one quilt show, there was a tired-looking lady with whom I spent some time talking. She confessed to being a "burned-out teacher," and said she didn't have energy for any new projects, although she admitted she loved Cathedral Window Quilting. She did buy a couple of small kits and about an hour later she came back ---face aglow and all excited. "Here! I found this fabric and I just *knew* you'd like it. I want you to have it! You have no idea what you've done for me. I feel as though I've been given a shot of adrenalin. Thank you!" I corrected her, "It wasn't me; it was the Lord reaching out to you." She quickly acknowledged she knew that. . . and from her glow, I knew she did.

Occasionally someone will tell me how much it meant to them when they spoke with me at a previous show. Often I do not remember the circumstances, and I now realize that at times like that, it is the Lord reinforcing me and filling *my* cup back up! That is to say, at times my human storehouse of provisions runs low, and He sends someone to replenish my supply. When I am weary, He provides strength for the journey, and I have learned that while He usually doesn't provide *in advance*, He does provide! It's kind of like this: He doesn't strap a huge gas pump onto my car, but He provides a station when I need one. His timing is incredible: He may not be early, but He is never late!

And as to the enigma about what He meant by "this will be good for Blairsville," there are a couple of young women who sew for me who would attest that this enabled them to be stay-at-home moms and earn the money they needed for their families. Once when I called Sue, one of the seamstresses, her little girl answered the phone and called excitedly to her mom in one breath, "It's-Arlene-Gray-can-I-get-new-shoes?!" When one of them hugs my neck and says, "I hope you know what a blessing you are for me," then the words of the Lord resound in my head and I am humbly grateful!

And just to prove that the Lord loves a good laugh, Sue recently told me a funny story. Her second-grader brought home a school test on which the following question was asked: "Who invented the sewing machine?" Her answer was: *"Arlene Gray."* She may not have done her homework in preparation for that test, but she knew that sewing was something that was important in her home, and Arlene Gray was involved in it. (Arlene Gray knows Who's *really* involved in it!)

The Lord Will Provide a Way
Where There Is No Way

After one of our trips to a two-day quilt show in Sarasota, Florida, Cheri and I faced a four hour drive home. But as a treat, I had bought tickets to a performance of the musical "Quilters" at the Asolo Theatre in Sarasota. It would mean that we would not arrive back home to Ft. Lauderdale until late, but I knew she would enjoy it, and the late night would be worth it.

Cheri was delighted, and we had a leisurely dinner before the performance began. It was a special evening, and Cheri got a chance to see the play that had been the catalyst for my beginning the quilting enterprise. She enjoyed it as much as I'd hoped she would, and I enjoyed it as much as I had the first two times.

As we prepared for the long drive home, we were talking about the play and recalling some of its poignant moments. Before we got onto "Alligator Alley," an 80-mile long stretch of desolate highway, I asked if we could stop for a restroom. Cheri said there was one at the toll-booth at the entry to the "Alley," so we stopped there. It was just after midnight.

As I was about to get out of the car, I suddenly hit my forehead with the palm of my hand and exclaimed, "No! Ohhhhhh, No!" Cheri asked what we had left behind (at the show), but I could only repeat, "No . . . no. . . noooooo!"

Finally, speech returned to me and I told her that I had forgotten to bring my gate-opener for the security gate at the mobile home park where I lived-- and Bill was up at the farm. She asked if I could call a neighbor to ask them to open the gate for me. I replied that since we wouldn't be arriving until after 2:00 a.m., I didn't think I could do that!

Cheri is usually level-headed and sharp-minded, but at that moment she was grasping for straws. "Then, could you call a neighbor now?" she asked. I was puzzled. "Why would I call a

115

neighbor *now?*" I asked. "Well, you could tell them you'd be calling them later to open the gate; then they wouldn't be so frightened when you called them back at 2:00 a.m."

As a recap, remember that it had been a long drive to the show, then set-up, then two long show days, and we were coming across the Alley after midnight. This didn't add up to two clear-thinking savvy women. But Cheri's suggestion--added onto all the other factors--really blew me out of the water, and I convulsed into a fit of laughing. I laughed so hard that tears streamed down my face, my nose started running, and I began coughing. As we pulled up to the toll-booth, the attendant looked past Cheri and asked, "Oh----uh, does she have allergies?" That was the straw that broke the camel's back, and by now I was laughing/crying/shaking all out of control.

When I caught my breath and was able to speak again, I told Cheri, "She doesn't think I have allergies . . . she thinks I'm high on drugs! And when she looked into the van packed with boxes, she probably thought we are running a big shipment across the state in the middle of the night. She's probably calling the highway patrol right now, so you better not speed, because we're probably on the Most Wanted List!"

We laughed all the way home. But when we got to my place, there loomed that formidable gate. And it appeared to have grown since I had left. Cheri asked, "What are you going to do?"

"I'm going to try to climb it," I replied. (I'm a grandmother--and not one who usually climbs gates. but there didn't seem to be a lot of options.) Cheri was concerned that I could get hurt. The two of us walked over to the gate and she pulled open a small opening between the two gates. She pulled one; I pushed the other, and a very, *very* small opening materialized. It didn't appear large enough for me to fit through, and I had visions of getting stuck part-way through and having to call for the emergency jaws of life to cut me out. But suddenly---though *humanly* impossible---I was through!

I walked (actually it was more like part skipped/part floated) the quarter-mile to my mobile home and when I got inside I pushed the gate-opener remote signal and Cheri drove through so we could unpack the car.

The *most* incredible part of the story, however, culminated in my discovery--about three days later--of some notes I had made in my Bible. As I thumbed through my Bible, a long notation along one margin and up across the top of the page caught my eye. I wondered what the lengthy note was in the margin of Proverbs 15:19 (The way of the sluggard is hemmed in as with thorns, but the path of the diligent is a highway). My handwritten note said, "Lord, sometimes your grace seems like I'm on a super highway--an interstate expressway! I'm in awe at the way you open doors for me to slip through (as though I were greased)!" What a strange thing for me to have written.

I don't recall writing it, and what is even stranger is the fact that I had dated it the very morning we had set off for our quilt show in Sarasota!   I very rarely date any notations I make in my Bible, but I know this was specifically dated so I would have evidence that the Lord was already prepared to "open doors for me to slip through as though I were greased!" His faithful word in Deuteronomy 1:30) tells us: "The Lord your God goeth before you. . ." And in this instance I believe He went before me carrying a gate-opener!

Be Alert: U-Turn Ahead!

I have learned to be open to opportunities that often require immediate decisions (and U-turns). So many times the Lord has allowed incredible experiences to unexpectedly enter my life, but for my part I must be willing to trust Him and walk in faith. Sometimes I have only a few days, a few hours---and once, only a few minutes---to make a decision and radically change direction. It's like those TV game shows where one is asked to decide between Curtains No. 1, No. 2, and No. 3, except that my willingness to be open to change has brought blessings that have far outweighed any mere TV prize.

For example, there was that early morning I was preparing to drive back to the farm after five days in Paducah, Kentucky for a quilt show. First I was going to drive Cheri to the Paducah airport for her return flight to Florida via a connection in St. Louis. Suddenly the phone rang. It was Bill, asking how the show had been and inquiring about my travel plans. He also said, "It's too bad that this isn't the year you were going to do the quilt show in Kansas City after Paducah." My ears perked up and I asked, "Why?" "Because a man from church needs someone to help him drive to Kansas City in a couple of days, and I could have met you there."

Wellll. . .! Kansas City is where my dear ole roommate Terri (that gal who wakes me up *early* whenever we get together) lives. I said I had to leave for the airport and would call him from there, and asked if he could get further details about when the man was leaving. I then called Terri and in a breathless run-on sentence said, "I know I woke you up, but what would you and Byron say if I showed up on your doorstep tonight, and don't answer because I don't have any details and I'll have to call you from the airport in Paducah in about thirty minutes, which should give you time to think up an excuse why this wouldn't work, okay? Bye."

When we got to the airport, we learned that Cheri's flight was overbooked and she had been bumped, with a six-hour wait until the next flight to St. Louis. I called Bill who gave me more specific information about leaving for Kansas City in two days; next I called

Terri and told her she'd have to put up with me for two days before Bill arrived. Then I threw in the clinker: "Terri, if I come, you will know beyond a shadow of a doubt that this was a totally unplanned trip, because all I have with me is a brown paperbag filled with five days' worth of dirty laundry!" She replied, "Come on ahead! We're about the same size and you can wear my clothes."

I looked at a map and started mentally planning a driving route. I realized that I would have to go right through St. Louis on my way to Kansas City. I asked Cheri if she'd like to drive with me to St. Louis and then take the next available flight home from there. She said she'd love to, and within minutes we were "On the Road Again. . ." So within less than thirty minutes from the time Bill said, "Too bad you're *not* going to Kansas City. . ." *we were on our way there, via St. Louis*!

As we approached St. Louis, the beautiful Gateway Arch loomed over the city and I asked Cheri if she'd ever been up in the Arch. She hadn't, and before one could say "Jackrabbit," we were high above the city, overlooking the vista below and marvelling aloud at the wonderment of it all and the provision of God.

I left Cheri at the airport and continued on to Kansas City, where I arrived about 8:00 p.m. We talked until midnight, and I know I must have looked mighty tired, because the next morning Terri, for the first time in our lives, let me sleep "late"---until 8:00 a.m! When I awoke, there was a little silver tray on the dressing table with orange juice and a fresh rose from the garden. It was just what my weary bones needed after a long, hard quilt show and travelling.

I put on my robe and went down to see if there were any clothes for me. Terri brought out a long-sleeved flannel shirt and bib-overall jeans, long socks to wear over the jeans legs, gardening gloves and a straw hat. I put the clothes on and told her to take my picture, because I wanted evidence for the lawsuit I was surely planning to file for cruel and inhuman treatment! (In fact, she and her husband had planned to go Morell mushroom-hunting and if I was to join them, my attire was requisite for the outing in order to avoid chiggers, ticks and spiders).

We had a wonderful two-day visit and the Lord filled the days with laughter and His special brand of joy. When Bill arrived he joined in the comraderie, and when my visit was over I felt revived and restored.

I marvelled at the fact that one minute I expected to be headed south to Georgia, and the next thing I knew I was going north to Kansas! And I thanked the Lord in wonderment at the way He had opened a surprising door for my refreshment and enjoyment. He is the God of breathtaking grace! And to think I could have missed it if I had dallied and not been alert and ready to walk through that doorway of opportunity. Lord, keep my spirit open and willing to change direction.

A Coincidence is a Miracle in Which
God Chooses to Remain Anonymous!

There are times in our lives when there is absolutely no denying that the hand of God is upon us---when there are so many "coincidences" that it is impossible not to believe that the Lord is involved. There have been such times in my life.

Even though I knew that the Lord wanted my trust in all circumstances, I was not prepared for His tender mercies when I faced having to sell our family home of 23 years in Florida. After all, I argued, it was---well, for lack of a better description---my nest; my "identity." Just because the children were grown and gone didn't seem a valid reason to let this precious (though large) house slip away, but my husband said we had to sell it, and I was hanging on for dear life.

For several months after it was listed with a realtor, I buried my head in the sand and refused to believe that a sale might be imminent, but finally I faced reality and fervently prayed that *if* a sale was part of His plan, the Lord would give me some sort of sign to reassure me. I also put a condition on it: the buyers had to have young children. If it were to sell, I wanted to know it was to the right family, that all the terms would be right and, knowing me as He does, that I would have sufficient time to prepare before a closing date.

The Lord has a marvelous sense of humor, and He is so gracious and merciful in times of stress. It shouldn't have surprised me when, two weeks after my prayer, a young couple with two little girls made us an all-cash offer to buy the house. I *knew* it was the "right" circumstances, because despite the difference in spelling, their name was "Wright"! They wanted the closing in *ten weeks* to coincide with the sale of their house--perfect timing for me to do my own sorting and packing.

One item that was causing some indecision was the piano on which our children had taken lessons. We offered it at half its value to the couple buying the house. At first they accepted, but because

123

they were also buying some of our furniture they decided against the piano. Again I implored the Lord to make the situation clear: I would make it available at its true value, and if it were meant to sell, then the Lord would provide a buyer (preferably one with a child about ten). A few days later during a garage sale, a man asked if I had any furniture to sell and I mentioned the piano. He said he'd bring his wife back to see it.

That afternoon he and his wife came with a petite girl whom I quickly "sized up" to be about seven. (Hmmm, is seven close to ten, Lord?) I asked how old she was. "Turning ten," she said. Still unconvinced, I wanted to know *when*. "In eight months." Close enough! They liked the piano and we agreed on terms. I asked the wife her name and when she told me my eyes got big as saucers and filled with tears. I hugged her and she said, "Oh, do you know me?" My reply was, "No, but this is *your* piano!" She was skeptical about how I could be so sure, and I told her the story about the couple who had bought our house after I had prayed for the "right" family. What was the name of the family who bought the piano? "Wright"--of course! (No relation to the Wrights who bought our house).

Now that we had sold our home, we were "homeless" and needed a small but convenient place to live during the winter months. My quilting business had become very active in Florida and I needed a home base from which to operate. It had to be easy to close up during the time we were in Georgia, operating the guest farm. We weren't sure where to look. We considered townhouses and apartments, but they didn't afford much privacy, storage space or gardening area. Next, we considered mobile homes and found a cheery double-wide on a canal. The people had moved and we were free to begin moving our belongings in.

There was a large tree on the neighboring property, for which I promptly gave thanks, "Lord, you know I need a big beautiful tree in my life, and even though this one isn't mine, I thank you for the shade of it anyway." A few days later as the property was surveyed ---lo and behold---the tree became "mine." The Bible says if we have the faith of a mustard seed we can command a mountain to go into the sea, but I had never seen a tree jump a property line before!

More evidence of His handiwork was in store. We had to have a new telephone number and our new exchange was to be 370. I asked the service rep if I could choose 1370 as the last four numbers. She checked its availability and said it wasn't in use but wouldn't be available for six weeks. I gasped and replied, "That's *exactly* when I want it!" I told her the "Wright-story" and even got a chance to witness about what 1370 means to me: "I serve **One** God in **Three** persons, **Seven** is His perfect number, and there is none-- **Zero**-- beside Him!"

When the lady from the moving company came to give us an estimate, she looked at the large home we were leaving and thought I might be having an emotionally hard time going to a mobile home. However, I assured her that this Little Tin Inn was the Wright-move for us, and we were in good (and Godly) hands! She said she was accustomed to most people weeping in similar circumstances and was amazed that I was so content.

And content I am. For I have learned that circumstances are not what bring happiness; joy is a gift for those who trust in God. Joy is different from happiness; it doesn't depend on circumstances, but comes from knowing the One who loves us and cares for us at all times. And I have also learned that He loves to surprise us with "coincidences" to prove His lovingkindness.

SNAFU . . . or SNIGH?

Timing is everything, isn't it? Knowing me as He does, the Lord realizes that if I know I have to deal with too many things at once I get discombobulated, so sometimes He simply keeps certain information "classified," until the proper time. Actually, I have been known to deal rather well under pressure. . . and conversely fall apart when I am given too much time to think.

In the middle of the big job of moving from our house of 23 years into our mobile home, I might have missed a wonderful visit from an out-of-town friend and an opportunity to spend time at the hospital in prayer for another dear friend, *if* I had known everything was going to happen at one time!

Let me back up a bit. My friend Angela had lab tests scheduled at the hospital on the 15th, and asked Gina and I to please go with her and pray during the procedure. My mom's doctor wanted to schedule an operation for her on the 17th. Other friends, Mary and her husband, were supposed to arrive in Florida and stay with us on the 22nd of the month. Things were starting to pile up, but it was still manageable. At least that's the way I thought it was supposed to go! But I was to learn the reality of my old boss' favorite saying: SNAFU (Situation Normal/All Fouled Up).

On the afternoon of the 15th, after seeing Angela's test come out with good results, I came home from the hospital and was on a telephone call when call-waiting announced another call. It was Mary. I told her I'd call her right back and asked if she was at work. There was a long, pregnant pause. "Uhm, no," she stammered, "Didn't you get my letter saying we would be arriving today? We're down the road and need directions." Then it was my turn to stammer, "Well, no, the letter I got said you'd be arriving a week from today. But this will work out fine; we'll just all go out to dinner and that will be a welcome break for me!"

They stayed a couple of nights and we had a great visit, but I know I would have been beside myself with worry and anxiety about the condition of the house if I'd known they were arriving *that* day. Also, I wouldn't have been able to give my undivided attention to Angela and her situation if I'd thought I was going to be receiving company a few hours later.

And it turns out that my mother's "scheduled" operation was actually a week later. The only thing she had to do on the 17th was a consultation with the surgeon. So you see, if Mary had come when she was originally scheduled, it would have been smack dab in the midst of Mom's operation. As it was, I was able to give Mom my undivided attention and be fully attentive during the time she needed me most.

After reflecting on how much discomfort I would have suffered regarding the condition of the house, I was reminded of a cute sign I once saw that said something like, "If you're coming to see my house, call for an appointment two weeks in advance; if you're coming to see me, drop in anytime!" What a reminder to keep things in perspective! I also remember reading a sign once that said "Angels can fly because they take themselves lightly." Lord, help me to remember that people are more important than things, and that I'm not to sweat the small stuff (and P.S.. it's mostly all small stuff!)

Mary said she couldn't believe how welcome I made her feel. And why not? She's a dear friend, and although she had said "Thursday" and given me a date a week later than she meant, it was a surprise---and a pleasant one---to have them with us a week early. In the Lord's wisdom, that "snafu" enabled me to be with my Mom for her operation the following week with nothing else on my schedule. Actually, it was a fitting end to my years in that house. The house got to play host one more time, and welcome guests under its roof in cordial hospitality as its final act.

I think this story deserves a really unique title, but I'd have to coin an entirely new word instead of SNAFU. Maybe the acronym could be SNIGH--which would stand for Situation Normal/In God's Hands!

Happy Birthday, Donald Duck

My youngest son Scott (then 16) and I took my father to Epcot Center to celebrate his 89th birthday. I was glad to have Scott along because Dad needed assistance that he would never allow a daughter to provide, and Scott had just the right measure of easy-going personality to fill the need without making Dad feel uncomfortable.

After we had been in the car for about fifteen minutes, Dad asked, "How much longer is it going to be?" I told him it was about a four hour trip, and he responded, "Oh, I never thought it would be that long!" Ten minutes later, he again asked how much longer. I told him to close his eyes and rest, and before he knew it we'd be there. Ten minutes later the scenario repeated itself. It was going to be a lonnnnnng trip.

Just before we arrived, I told Dad that it might be a good idea to get a wheelchair but he interrupted me, "I've never been in a wheelchair and I'm not getting in one now! Absolutely not!"

"Well, Dad," I said, "How about we get one and you just try it out for ten minutes? If you don't like it, you can get out. And I'll get in and you can push me, because wheelchairs go to the front of the lines and they don't have to wait . . . What do you say?"

A slow, sheepish grin crossed his face and he decided he'd go along with the plan--but just to avoid the lines, mind you.

He had a wonderful time, laughing and enjoying all the new-fangled inventions and fascinating exhibits. He particularly enjoyed the exhibit of hydroponics and couldn't get over the fact that vegetables were growing out of little vials of water, and the produce was hanging down heavily-laden. We had lunch at the French pavillion and he reminisced about his boyhood in Paris before coming to the U.S. at the age of seven. We went to the photo studio and donned old-fashioned clothes for a tin-type memento of an era gone by. And did I mention that we laughed---a lot?

I bought him a Donald Duck hat with a big orange bill sticking out as a visor. We took dozens of pictures and stayed late to watch the fireworks. On the boat ride back to the main entrance at the end of a long day, a little boy looked at Dad wearing his duck-hat and just stared at him. Dad smiled; the boy stared. The more Dad tried to get a response from the little tyke, the more he stared back blankly. Dad had a fit of laughing and nearly lost his breath. It was a memorable November day. It was his last birthday. But it was a gift . . . even more for me than for him. And I shall never forget our final celebration together and how the Lord provided two perfect days to erase some of the rough times when there had been misunderstandings rather than laughter. It reminds me of the promise in Psalm 30 that says "weeping may endure for a night, but joy cometh in the morning." Praise God for His joy that erases the times of weeping.

Choices . . . and Blessings

Two weeks after my Dad's 89th birthday, we got a call from Bill Jr. who was away at college. He said he had an opportunity to go to Japan for Christmas with his roommate whose father was a colonel in the Air Force and stationed there. He asked if we'd mind his missing Christmas with the family. I knew that my Dad---his Poppy---held a special place in Billy's heart, so I told him that I had seen Poppy losing ground over the past several months and that this would probably be his last Christmas. I told him I wasn't saying he couldn't or shouldn't go, but just giving him information that I thought he might want to have.

Billy opted to come home that year. He and Poppy enjoyed their visit together, and Poppy laughed long and hard at him, especially when Billy put on all the ski-gear we had bought him--- pants, jacket, scarf, hat, face mask, goggles, gloves---and then came out walking like an overstuffed monster.

It had been a hard decision for an 18-year-old to make, considering that the opportunity for the trip to Japan might not come to him again, but less that two months later Poppy passed away. When we called Billy at school, we told him it would not be necessary for him to come back for the funeral since he had been here with Poppy when he needed him. (And P. S. a mere three years later Billy was stationed in Japan for two years and in Korea for one year, and missed Christmas with the family three years in a row.)

Dad was cremated, and neither my mother nor my brother wanted to go back to the funeral home for the ashes. I said I'd go. On the morning I was going to pick up Dad's ashes, I went to work until noon. Sharon, who had been my friend since high school, called me at work and asked how I was doing. I said, "I'm all right; I'm only working until about lunchtime and then I'm going to get Dad's ashes and scatter them in the Bay that he loved so much. She asked who was going with me. "No one," I replied. "But I'll be all right." She absolutely insisted on meeting me at the funeral home. That was a godsend, because I hadn't realized how emotionally charged and difficult that moment would be.

We drove out to Biscayne Bay and suddenly I was aware of how incredibly heavy I felt. I was unable to pray or read the Scriptures, so Sharon did both for me. As I knelt down on the wooden dock and prepared to pour the ashes out, I felt like I weighed five hundred pounds. However, as I started pouring them, I got lighter and lighter until I began to think I was going to float up into the sky like a helium balloon . . . and I wondered if Sharon would notice and grab my leg as I went soaring up!

Suddenly it seemed that I could see each individual sparkle on the water, that I had never seen the sun so golden, that I could hear each bird singing a unique song, and that the breathtaking beauty of the scene was unparalleled in my memory. After a while, Sharon asked if I wanted to get something to eat. We drove over to a little outdoor cafe on the Bay and I remember having a fresh fruit salad that was the sweetest, freshest, most succulent food I had ever tasted. It was a puzzlement. I had just scattered my Dad's ashes, and yet I was filled with heightened sensitivities I had never experienced before--(nor have I ever experienced since). I couldn't comprehend what was happening and it only lasted about an hour. But I believe it was tangible evidence that my heavenly Father had not abandoned me as I dealt with burying my earthly father! The Lord took the burden I was carrying and replaced it with His peace. In the words of Jesus (Matthew 5:4), I experienced the healing touch of the Lord just as He had promised: "Blessed are they that mourn; for they shall be comforted."

Give Thanks in All Circumstances

Sometimes we come upon a verse in Scripture that doesn't seem to make sense. How could one possibly give thanks in *all* circumstances? Other verses in Scripture serve to illuminate the situation into its proper perspective . . .but I'm getting ahead of my story.

Many years ago I learned a lesson that made an indelible mark on me. At the end of a long day's shopping excursion encompassing about six or seven stores over a forty-mile distance, I discovered that I had lost my birthstone ring which had been given to me by my father, who had passed away a few months earlier.

After several unsuccessful attempts to find it at the various stores I had shopped in, I returned to our farm. Driving through the mountains in the encroaching darkness, I was feeling quite disconsolate indeed. I sensed the Lord urging me to sing the song, "Praise Him in the morning....praise Him in the noontime...." and I thought, "I will, but I just don't feel like it right now." He was insistent, however, and indicated that despite my feelings I was just to do it. I reluctantly complied and began to sing rather softly. After a few minutes I was singing with gusto, and through tears of gratitude I found myself praising Him for many things: "Thank you for the ring. Thank you that it had been beautiful. Thank you that it had been a gift from my father as tangible evidence of his love." I released the ring in perfect peace and experienced a healing sense of peace and comfort instantly.

As I walked up the hill to the farmhouse in the dark and reached for the doorknob, I felt a little piece of paper taped to the door. I turned on the light and read, "If you lost a ring, call this number." *If I lost a ring, call this number*?! How could this note have gotten here? I was at a farm in a remote area (with no telephone at the time), and somehow, somewhere, someone had left this message for me. And yes, I *did* get my ring back---but even more profound was the realization that the Lord had asked me to sing a praise song *before* I found out that the ring would be returned to me! That was a lasting lesson that He desires my praise and obedience in *all* circumstances---not just when He does what I want.

There have been times when praising Him has come automatically, and times when it has been difficult, but He taught me the meaning in the Scripture of "the sacrifice of praise." In answer to my questioning him about this phrase, He explained that, "When you are devoid of any reason to praise Me--- if, indeed, you will praise Me *then*---it is like the sweetest incense to My nostrils and I will bless you." And He has been faithful in this regard. I have received both physical and emotional healings when I was obedient to the mandate to "Give Thanks in All Circumstances." That doesn't mean I am "happy" about the circumstances; it just means that I remember that giving the Lord the honor and praise He deserves is paramount in the situation.

Some years after I independently learned this lesson, I read a powerful book by Merlin Carouthers, entitled *The Power in Praise*. It is a dynamic and powerful book that relates the stories of many people whose personal testimony substantiates this basic truth. I wholeheartedly recommend this book for further clarification of the blessings that come from obediently giving praise to the Lord. However, it would be sheer folly to think that merely mouthing praise is a means of providing a "miracle." No; God desires our *trust* in all situations and our confidence that He is in control. From that basic tenet springs our ability to praise Him in all circumstances.

I have learned to trust Him and praise Him even in seemingly impossible situations *because of Who He is*, and not for what I "expect" Him to do. But I never ceased to be surprised by the blessings and "coincidences" that come my way as I lean on His everlasting arms!

A Friend Loveth At All Times

There is a type of friendship that crosses all boundaries into a special realm. When one has a friend who is also a prayer-partner, then the pinnacle of personal friendship has been reached. Cathy was that type of heart-to-heart friend to me for many years in Blairsville. She faithfully met with me on a weekly basis to pray and search God's word for direction, and she never let me "get away with" any excuses or rationalizations. At the same time, equalizing the scales in perfect balance, she loved me with unconditional love.

Cathy was a warm and wonderful woman, the mother of six, grandmother to nearly a dozen, and great-grandmother to a precious new arrival that rounded out their family's circle. At one point in her marriage, she and her husband Charlie had been separated for several years, but neither sought other mates and both felt that if the Lord intended marriage for them, then it would be with the one they had pledged vows to years earlier.

Cathy's marriage was restored and she said that the Lord had filled her with a renewed and vibrant love for her husband, and that He had washed away the hurts and pain of the past, and replaced them with His love.

Whenever I expressed my own frustrations or hurts she always found Scripture that soothed with a healing balm, and she always encouraged me never to give up hoping and trusting in the Lord for the answers. Her words to me were always from the Word of Truth, and included such admonitions as Trust; Stand Secure; Resist; Never Forget We're On the Winning Side; A Mighty Fortress Is Our God; Never-failing. And she reminded me that the Lord had said He "would restore the years the locust has eaten." In short, Cathy was a super-encourager.

Cathy was a talented seamstress with a creative bent. She was fully a Lady in every sense of the word, in a world that has forgotten what that revered title should mean. She delighted in providing a warm and cozy home for her husband, in hosting visiting members of her family, and in entertaining a small circle of friends. She always provided unique little touches, like lace doilies and porcelain teacups, and small vases filled with wildflowers, to make people feel special.

She also knew the winding backroads of the Georgia mountain countryside like the back of her hand. Sometimes we'd set off on a "road-rally"---as our husbands referred to our expeditions---to find a fabric shop in some barn or out-of-the-way locale. We would picnic along the way and get back barely in time to make supper for our menfolk. I specifically remember how many stores we visited when she was looking for fabric to make the coordinating bedspread, dustruffle, pillows, curtains and shower curtain for the house they had recently moved into. The prints included violets, ivy and matching stripes, and when she finished making all the items, it was a bedroom that was worthy of a centerfold spread in *House Beautiful*.

She wasn't particularly good about keeping up with correspondence, however, and during the months I was in Florida she was always apologizing for being tardy in her letter-writing. One icy cold January day, however, Bill and I had to make a whirlwind drive up to Blairsville to pick up something from the farm and return to Florida the very next day. While in Blairswville, I called Cathy and she was surprised to learn that I was in town. She said, "You're not going to believe this, but there's a letter in the mail, and you'll get it when you get back home!" She wanted to know whether (since I had made the telephone call to her), she now owed me *another* correspondence! And we had a good laugh over that. All the way home during that twelve hour drive I was buoyed by the bubbly and happy conversation we had shared. Never did I suspect that it would be our last conversation.

A few weeks later, on a snowy February evening, with Cathy driving her car and her husband following behind in his truck, they came up and over Neel's Gap on their way home. A car passed Cathy's husband and got between their two cars, and Charlie lost sight of Cathy's car in the low visibility of the swirling snow and the twisting and turning road. When he reached the bottom of the mountain, there was no sign of Cathy. He knew she would have pulled over and waited for him there, but he was alone on the road.

136

He called 911 for emergency help, but when they went back up, there were only tire tracks going off the top of the mountain. Down in the ravine was my beloved friend and prayer-partner. That is to say, her earthly body was there. She had soared off in midair to meet her Lord and Savior in the clouds.

When I got the news, I was totally disconsolate. Some days after her funeral, I called her dear son, Charles Jr., who was like a son to me as well, and I wept unabashedly. Charles was tender and compassionate with me and allowed me to ventilate my feelings of loss and deprivation. Although I should have been bringing comfort to him, in fact, he gently helped me work through my own emotions and bereavement. He quoted some Scripture to me and helped me get my feet planted back on solid ground---on the Solid Rock, that is.

The next day as I was seeking a Word from the Lord, I expected some words like "they who mourn shall be comforted," and was surprised to receive the words from Nehemiah 8:10: "Do not be saddened this day, for rejoicing in the Lord must be your strength." And as the day wore on, I discovered a joy that I didn't think I would experience again, at least not for a long time!

Two days later, however, was Valentine's Day, and the enemy slipped in to help me create a pity-party. I started thinking, "Why did it have to be Cathy who died---she had so many people who loved her and will miss her; why couldn't it have been me? Who would miss me, anyway? Et cetera, et cetera, ad nauseum! (I'm the queen of pity-parties, and can throw one with the best of them).

With these thoughts in mind, I was driving to the post office in a drizzly rain, and with the rain plop-plop-plopping on my windshield, it seemed that even God was crying that day. As I approached the post office counter, the postal lady asked, "How are you today, Arlene?" Well, the poor dear never knew what hit her, because I started bawling out loud. I muttered something about the loss of a dear friend and left as quickly as I could. That day the Lord allowed me to find two special letters among my mail, affirming the importance of my friendship to two people I hadn't expected to hear from. It occurred to me that while it was Valentine's Day when I had received the correspondence in answer to my cry of petition, the Lord had prompted those folks to write two days earlier (as attested to by the postmarks). Therefore, the answer to my plea arrived on the very day when I was most in need! Talk about time management!

Some months later, when Cathy's husband had sold their house and was preparing to move the last of his belongings out, I stopped over to see if I could help in any way. Charles Jr. asked if I might be interested in purchasing the large bedroom set that had been Cathy and Charlie's, but it was too big to fit in our farmhouse. The beautiful violet- and ivy-strewn fabric that Cathy had so lovingly and carefully selected for the bedspread and the pilllows filled the room with Cathy's touch, and I asked if the spread and curtains might be for sale. Charles Jr. said they would be pleased if I could use them, and my eyes filled with tears to be able to have a material remembrance of Cathy for my own. He also gave me a photo of an oil painting of Cathy and Charlie that had been painted several years earlier. She was a rather shy and self-conscious person, despite her obvious good looks, and rarely allowed anyone to take her photo, so I was very pleased to have such an attractive likeness of her.

At the farmhouse, in the upstairs bedroom, there is a beautiful room that oozes the essence of my friend Cathy. There is an aura of quietness and peace about the room, and I believe the Lord allowed me to have this visible reminder of this precious and dear prayer-partner. Whenever I see it, I am grateful for the warm memories of a very special friendship with a very special lady. Cathy continually pointed the way to the One who would love me most, even when I was deprived of one of whom it could be said, "A friend loveth at all times." And I know that in times of loss or need, she would have aimed my focus on "the One who sticks closer than a brother."

I besought the Lord to bring another powerful prayer warrior into my life. Several weeks after Cathy's death, at the end of a women's Bible study meeting at my Ft. Lauderdale church, someone came up behind my chair, put her hands on my shoulders, leaned over and whispered in my ear, "Do you have a prayer partner?" I didn't know who it was . . . but I surely knew Who had sent her!

Peace That Passes All Human Understanding

I had driven my husband to the airport in Atlanta from our farm. It is a two-hour drive each way, and I had done some shopping and run some errands after dropping him off. I was hungry, but I discovered I didn't have so much as a dollar on me. However, I faced a long drive home, and needed to eat something before starting back.

Because I had to go to a restaurant where I could use a credit card, I was considerably delayed starting home. It was after 9:00 p.m., much later than I had planned to start the two-hour trip, and I was acutely aware of how tired I was.

For the first hour or so, there was a fair amount of traffic-- which provided enough stimulus to keep me alert. However, when I was only about fifteen minutes from home, there were no cars on the dark road, and I could feel my eyes growing bleary as the curves and hills lulled me into sleepiness.

I was so sound asleep when I hit the ditch that I was not even aware that I was driving, even though my foot was still on the gas pedal and I was travelling at 65mph! The next thing I knew, I was hurtling pell-mell through a deep ditch, and signs were coming at me: "Do Not Enter, Do Not Enter." I remember thinking, "Who would *want* to enter?!" I had no control of the car and as the reality of the situation became clear, the thought that crossed my mind was, "Oh. . . so this is how it's going to end."

Then the car veered toward the guardrail and I thought, "Awww, just like Cathy" (my faithful prayer-partner who was killed when her car went off the top of a mountain during a snowstorm a year earlier). Suddenly the car straightened out and came to an abrupt stop, hurtling everything toward the front of the car. A heavy object fell on my right foot, and as I looked down I saw that it was my cellular phone. I heard a gentle message, "You're okay . . . call for help."

So many things went through my mind. First, I was amazed that at the very moment I had thought "Oh, so this is how it's going to end," I was aware of an incredible sense of calm. It was almost as though I had thought, "Oh, it's Thursday." I also thought about the cell-phone. For nearly two years my sons had been paying the monthly bill to provide me with the phone, and I had often complained at the waste of money it was. I would ask, "Do I look like a cell-phone type of person? Can you picture me driving down the highway and calling in an order for 10,000 shares of stock or 200 head of cattle?" Nevertheless, they said that since I travel extensively with my quilting business, it might come in handy in an emergency. For two months it had been sitting idle, uncharged. But the night before I drove to the airport I decided to charge it and put it in the car. (Do you believe in "coincidences"?)

The sheriff answered my 911-call and came out to the highway. Before he arrived, I walked around the car to assess the situation. It had rained for two days prior to this incident, turning the Georgia soil to mirey-clay. Since the ditch was filled with thigh-high weeds, every crack and crevice of my car was embedded with clay and long, hairy weeds. It looked like an all-terrain vehicle that had seen some fierce action! I pulled about ten pounds of weed-embedded clay from the under-carriage of the car before the sheriff arrived. One of the rear tires was off the axle and it appeared that the axle may have been broken. But I was not injured (except for the bruise on my foot where the cell-phone had hit it and a serious rug-burn on my elbow where it had vigorously scraped back and forth on the armrest as I wrestled with the steering wheel), and I was grateful that I was still in one piece.

When the tow truck arrived, the driver didn't think he could put the spare on the axle, but--lo and behold--he could! He said he'd tow my car and drive me home. It was the same tow truck mechanic mentioned in the story about my car being disabled at the top of the mountain--Wayne--(we were now on a first-name basis). I said I thought I could drive home, but he said, "You can't! We don't know what damage was done to the underside, and it wouldn't be safe for you to drive the car in this condition until it gets checked out." But I

140

said that if I didn't feel safe I wouldn't drive it, and if he would just follow behind me, I would pull right over if I didn't have confidence about it. Reluctantly, he followed me about seven miles to the turn-off for my road to the farm, and I pulled over and thanked him. He was incredulous that the car could operate as it did.

The next day I took the car to be checked out up on the rack. Seeing the mud-encrusted condition of the exterior of the car, the mechanic was also surprised that there was just some minor wheel misalignment which he was able to fix while I waited. I then went to the tire store to replace the mangled-looking tire, but after cleaning and checking the old tire, it needed only a couple of weights to restore it to serviceability. (It reminded me of how I often need to be "cleaned up and checked" before being restored to serviceability, and I am grateful that I know a Service Master even better than Mr. Goodwrench.)

Later I returned to the site where the incident had occurred the night before. I looked at the skid marks and was amazed at the distance they covered, evidence of how long I travelled without being in control of my car. I measured them . . . over five hundred feet!

I realized that something more than the preservation of my life had occurred. I knew that I had been healed of fear, anxiety, worry and nervousness. I was aware that following an incident like that, many people would never have driven again, but on the contrary, I felt confident enough to have driven cross-country--right then!

After confessing to the Lord my regret for taking His protection so for granted, and admitting that I had acted in an irresponsible manner, I gave him praise and thanksgiving for His faithfulness in being my provider and for healing me of fears and nervousness that had plagued me in my earlier years. For me, it was far more awesome to have been healed of these debilitating reactions than merely that my life had been somehow spared. It was evidence that I am a new creation in Christ! Praise God! Isaiah 26:3 says, "Thou wilt keep him in perfect peace, whose mind is stayed on thee: because he trusteth in thee." Lord, keep my mind stayed on Thee!

Now That I Am Old and Gray

Once I was young and Gray. In fact, the first time I introduced Bill to my mother, she noted how gray his hair was, though he was just in his 30's. He replied, "I've been Gray since birth." She didn't catch on for a few minutes, but later it was a favorite family joke.

Now, however, I am older and Gray. And one of the benefits of age is the opportunity to be seen as "wise" or "learned" or "experienced" by the younger women. I love the relationships I have with young mothers as they sort out their own parenting role and seek to follow the Lord's direction in raising His children.

Several years ago, one of our guest families at the farm consisted of Jane and Eddie and their five little children--the youngest of whom celebrated his 6-weeks' birthday at the farm. I was impressed with them at first sight. Jane home-schooled her children and seemed to have her priorities in order, and Eddie was an attentive dad.

Eddie's arms were covered with tattoos, and I remarked, "What a strong witness for the Lord you must be with all those tattoos!" He looked puzzled and said he had gotten the tattoos before he became a believer. I smiled and said I assumed as much but it appeared that he must have had a very different lifestyle at one time. He still looked puzzled and said that was true, but that the Lord had come into his life and had changed him. However, he said most people looked at the tattoos and wondered how he could be a Christian. "Oh," I replied, "that's because they're looking at the tattoos, and not at *you*!"

In the middle of their stay, I heard the message: "Jane is your daughter; and one day, Christy will be Jane." I realized that it was the Lord's reassurance that young Christy would one day be the mature woman of God that Jane is. It was a reassuring promise from the One whose promises are faithful. The next day I told Jane about the message that she was "my daughter." She looked surprised but after reflection and prayer, she shared her thoughts with me. She said that she had prayed for a mother- and grandmother-figure for her family, and here was I fulfilling that role! At the time, Jane didn't live anywhere near me or any of my relatives, and I wondered how I'd ever see her again. Nevertheless, we began corresponding and I got to know her better. About two years later (coincidentally?), my daughter moved to within a thirty-minute drive of Jane, so whenever I visit Christy, I can also visit Jane as well! Over the past several years, I have been gifted with many happy get-togethers with her and her children, who call me Gran'ma Gray.

It was Jane who taught me how to do sponge-painting. I put my newly acquired art skills to work on a wall in our Little Tin Inn in Ft. Lauderdale. Everyone who has seen it thinks it is absolutely beautiful, and it is a lasting reminder that we rarely are called to *give* in any situation when we are not also on the receiving end.

At our church in Blairsville, there is a program called "Heart-to-Heart," which pairs up older women with young mothers. My partner is Rachel, a lovely young woman with five children, who also home-schools them. She's a terrific gal and a great bread baker, and I have reaped the benefits of her baking skills on many occasions. I also was able to take my new sponge-painting talent and help her create a garden scene in her daughters' bedroom.

The Bible teaches us some things about growing older. Verse 18 of Psalm 72, says: "Now that I am old and gray, O God, forsake me not, til I proclaim your strength to every generation that is to come." And Titus 2:4 tells us, "By their good example they (older women) must teach the younger women to love their husbands and children, to be sensible, chaste, busy at home, kindly, and submissive to their husbands." It is silent on the many *benefits* that accrue to those who are obedient to these instructions. In the process I was taught art skills and received freshly baked bread. And lots of hugs from lots of chill'uns. And notes like this: "Arlene, may you be blessed with encouragement like you've given to me. Your prayers have lifted me from despair many times, and your loving confrontation has turned me around. Thank you for sharing your wisdom, your talents and your time with my family." Whew! Talk about blessings!

He Heals the Broken-hearted
and Binds Up Their Wounds

Did you ever have "one of those days ..." one that seemed more like a year? There was a movie titled "48 Hours" that was touted to be a rip-snorting, hair-raising, heart-pounding adventure. We've all had our share of "48 Hours," but there was one that topped all others for me.

My daughter, her husband, six-year old Stephanie and four-year old Brandon had all suffered through a messy bout with a virus and I was glad to hear that they were finally on the mend. Two days later, however, the phone rang and Christy said that Stephanie had several black-and-blue marks on her and she couldn't account for them. Christy feared that child abuse would be suspected and that the authorities would take Stephanie into "protective custody." However, the next day there were also some little specks of red on Stephanie's skin, so Christy took her to the doctor.

The doctor said the specks were a sign of internal bleeding and ordered a blood test immediately. The normal blood platelet level ranges from 140,000-440,000, and Stephanie's was at a *critical* 6,000. The doctor said that if Stephanie bumped her head she could have bled to death internally! The phone call from Christy ended with her saying the doctor arranged for a bone marrow test to rule out leukemia, and she was going directly to an oncologist/ hematologist. She said, "Pray, and call others to pray, too."

I was at the farm in Georgia; they were in St. Petersburg. The 600 miles separating us seemed like a continent apart. At first I was in shock, unable to even think. Then I started calling members of the prayer chain at church, as well as some friends I knew to be prayer warriors. I got answering machines, no answers, and that annoying sound that announces that the computer is on-line. Finally I reached the husband of one of the prayer chain members, who said his wife would be home in a couple of hours and he'd be sure to give her my message. After various unsuccessful attempts to get prayer in motion, I was frustrated and felt like my insides were exploding within me.

I wanted to pray, but I was immobilized. I desperately called out to the Lord and told Him how much I missed my old prayer partner/mentor Cathy, especially at a time like this. I needed someone to pray with me and to help jump-start my own prayer that was locked deep in the dungeon of my soul. I was nearly frantic. Suddenly the deafening silence was broken by the ringing of the telephone. It was Mary Clare and David from Tampa, who had twice stayed at our guest farm and whom I knew to be prayer warriors. They called to say they were in Blairsville and had bought some property and wanted to stop by. My voice broke as I told them about Stephanie and asked them to please come.

They were at my door within a few minutes and as they hugged me, I felt the Lord's comforting and healing touch instantaneously. Their daughter had had Hodgkin's Disease a couple of years earlier, and Mary Clare (who is a nurse) prayed that Stephanie would be admitted to All-Children's Hospital and have the same oncologist/hematologists who had helped her daughter. Here I had been wondering how/where/what--*and from a town neighboring my daughter's*, came reassurance and a sense of order! We prayed for about fifteen minutes or so, and at last I was able to release the praise and worship to the Lord that had been locked within me. As we finished praying, I felt a peace that simply *cannot* be explained. As soon as our prayer ended, the phone rang. It was Christy; they were at the very hospital Mary Clare had mentioned, under the care of the oncologist/hematologist group she had spoken of. What a confirmation that Stephanie was where she was supposed to be! Christy said the initial tests had ruled out leukemia, and that it seemed to be a reaction of Stephanie's immune system which ---after attacking the virus she had had---continued on a search-and-destroy mission and wiped out her platelets, too.

Christy said they expected Stephanie to be in the hospital for four days. The hospital would allow Christy (*and* Brandon) to stay overnight with Stephanie, since Keith was the night crew manager at

146

work. Allowing Brandon to stay was a remarkable arrangement, since four-year olds are not usually allowed to even be visitors in hospitals, and I was glad Stephanie would have her mommy there because I knew that would aid in the healing process. She would be hooked up to intravenous, but the news was infinitely better than it had been a few hours earlier!

I realized that although I had been unsuccessful in getting the prayer chain started, the Lord was working through the unspoken groanings of my heart. Then the phone rang again. It was the woman in charge of the prayer chain, on whose answering machine I had left a rather incoherent message. She said she had *already* heard about it on a second line of the chain while she was in town. It seems the lady's husband I had spoken to earlier decided he wouldn't wait for his wife to get home and had started the chain himself! So, unbeknownst to me, *others had in fact been praying.*

And remember my crying out earlier to the Lord that I really missed my prayer partner Cathy's presence in this situation? Well, David said they had stopped by to see Cathy's son Charlie when they got to Blairsville. David and Charlie both compose music and had formed a friendship, rooted in their mutual love of the Lord. And when David asked if Charlie knew whether the Grays were in town, it was my dear *Cathy's son* Charlie whose finger dialed my number and handed the phone to Mary Clare! I don't believe in coincidences.

The next morning, Christy said Stephanie's platelet level had gone from 6,000 to 18,000 overnight and that was a good sign, but she was still in serious condition. The doctor said if the level tripled again the next day, they might consider allowing her to go home after the second day. That meant that 54,000 was the number to aim for. The next day, her level didn't triple, nor did it quadruple, nor multiply by five or even six times. No, it was a very surprised doctor who discovered that it had risen by nearly *seven*fold--to a nearly low-normal rate of 120,000! He said to Stephanie, "Whoa! How did you do *that*? You must have really wanted to go home badly, eh?"

Christy told me of another sign of the Lord's intervention in this matter. Christy does daycare in her home, taking care of babies through the county's program for teenage mothers so they can continue going to school. Two days prior to all the events related above, Christy had received a visit from a home health care inspector, who noted that Stephanie needed an updated physical immunization record (a requirement for keeping her daycare license), and Christy was given ten days to comply with that stipulation. She said that she is so grateful for that mandate because she might have overlooked the urgency of Stephanie's bruises. However, since she had to go to the doctor anyway, it forestalled any delay that might have proven disastrous! Christy said it was like the Lord *required* her to go to the doctor. Afterwards, Christy posted some information on the Internet alerting parents to the warning signs of bruises, and received lots of positive comments and commitments of prayer from many people around the world. She said the feedback and support felt like "reinforcements in the battle."

Stephanie left the hospital on a Wednesday, but still seemed to be having some side effects from the procedures she'd endured. She was bloated and nauseous. On Thursday night I got a phone call from Christy saying they were heading to the emergency room. She had been in contact with the doctor who suspected aseptic meningitis, but not the life-threatening form. Christy was at the emergency room all night, but Friday morning she sounded confident, secure and composed. She had opted not to let the E.R. perform a spinal tap. My first reaction was that that was a mistake, but as I listened to my daughter's explanation I realized what an alert, mature and competent mother she had become. She explained, "There were absolutely no indications that the dangerous form of meningitis was involved, and it is too risky to subject a child to a treatment that could potentially paralyze her." Her doctor said she had made a proper judgment!

When they left the next morning, Stephanie's platelet count was all the way up to 230,000, and by that night she was her happy, bubbly, giggly self again. Christy told Stephanie that because she had missed rehearsals all week, she'd lost her part in the professional ballet company's production of "Alice In Wonderland," but her response was, "Oh, well, that's okay; when's the next show?" What a trouper!

As this is written, on the day after the interminable "48 Hours," I have been reflecting on the incredible grace and mercy of the Lord. In my inability to pray, He provided His own prayer-warriors! In accord with Psalm 147:3, He took my achy-breaky heart and healed it, and bound up my wounded spirit, as well as Stephanie's mixed-up immune system. As it says in Deuteronomy 1:30, "The Lord your God which goes before you, He *Himself* shall fight for you." And when I was unable to fend for myself, that's just what He did; He stepped in for me!

When I called my friend Lucy in Florida and told her about the chain of events, she said, "Wow! God really *is* awesome, isn't He?" (She always chastises me for using the word "awesome" too often in my description of God!) Lucy, forgive me, but just once more I *have* to say it: The Lord is an *awesome* God!

Fasten Your Seatbelt for the Rollercoaster Ride!

We've all had mountaintop experiences, and we've all experienced wandering in the desert. A rollercoaster ride is both of those experiences sandwiched together and alternately going one direction and immediately in the other, and then repeated, over and over again. It leaves you breathless. The only thing that holds you together is being securely fastened. At times like that, I am ultimately grateful for the all-powerful arms of the Lord to hold me together as the altitude changes rapidly and the bottom drops out. After the "48 Hours" came the rollercoaster ride.

The days dragged into interminable weeks, as Stephanie's platelet count fluctuated up and down like a yo-yo. Whenever she wore socks, her ankles would get all black-and-blue from the elastic, and where her six-year molar was cutting through, there was evidence of internal bleeding from the pressure. Up and down. Up and down. It never went back to the critical level at which it had first been discovered, and we were grateful that the fluctuations were within a fairly acceptable---though low---range. Nonetheless, its constant recurrence kept us all before the Throne.

Then sixty days from the onset, the phone rang, and I heard the most beautiful words that a six-year old could utter, "Gran'ma, God healed my ITP!" ("ITP" stands for a medical diagnosis that I cannot pronounce, much less spell). Not only was I grateful for the physical healing, but even more important, I was supremely grateful for that child's grasp of the Lord's touch on her life! Never once throughout her ordeal did I ever hear her complain, whine or grumble (like I would have done when I was six years old!). I pray that wherever her life's journey takes her, she will always be aware that her hand is in His hand, and that when she is too weary, He will carry her. As her pronouncement echoed over the telephone wires, I realized that the rollercoaster ride had come to a halt. It was time to get off and be grateful for the Firm Foundation to stand on. The Rock of Ages is, indeed, a solid place to anchor in times of need!

Several weeks later when Stephanie and her family came up to the farm for a visit, I received another once-in-a-lifetime thrill. At church, that Sunday, the pastor asked if there were any visitors to be introduced, and when I raised my hand he asked, "Arlene, who do you have with you today?" I told him I had an entire row: a family from Florida who was staying at our cabins, and my daughter and her family. The pastor remembered that the church had prayed for my granddaughter and he asked how she was. Christy said, "She is doing well. Would it be all right for her to come up and say something?"

My head rubber-necked as I looked over to see what was going on. I had no idea this was "in the plan." And I didn't think my granddaughter was outgoing enough to be able to speak in front of hundreds of people. But I was wrong. Christy asked Stephanie if she wanted her mommy to go up to the altar with her, but Stephanie said simply, "No," and marched down the long aisle to the pastor. She took the hand-microphone from him, turned toward the congregation and said, "I just want to thank everybody for praying for me when I was sick. I'm better now." With that, she handed back the mike, turned, and walked down the aisle to where her grandmother was sitting with jaw open in wide-eyed wonder! Lord, Your tender mercies are new every morning, and I praise and bless You for the grateful heart You have planted in this precious grandchild.

And the Lord Shall Provide . . .

While Stephanie was in the hospital, I wondered how I could get a small gift to her and I felt led to call my friend Jane (the one of whom the Lord had said "she is your daughter"), who lived about an hour away from the hospital. I asked if there was any way she could pick up some small gifts and bring them over to Stephanie "from Gran'ma and Gran'pa." I knew it was a rather presumptuous request, both from time-scheduling and financial standpoints. But the Lord's hand was definitely in the request *and* in the fulfillment.

Jane bought some various items and brought them to the hospital, and when I later asked to repay her, she said, "Arlene, it is so seldom in our financial circumstances that I have an opportunity to do works of mercy, that it was a true blessing. Let me tell you what happened. I had been setting aside some money for a schoolbook for one of the children, and the night before I spoke to you I was at church and felt led to give about a third of it to a missionary cause. Then the next morning when you called, I wondered how I could spare the money, but I stepped out in faith and obedience and used over half of what was left to buy the items for Stephanie. I then had only a small fraction left for the book I needed. That very day a friend called to tell me that someone had a used book for sale, but I didn't think I had anywhere near enough for even a used book. But in the Lord's providence, I had exactly the amount the woman wanted! So please don't reimburse me, or I will have lost the blessing of experiencing the Lord's provision in times of need!" *Isn't that a wonderful illustration of the Great Provider?*

I needed to fly down to Florida to see Stephanie with my own eyes. I ordered a pretty doll that looked like her to be shipped to me by express-mail, so I could bring it with me. Prior to the events which culminated with my making flight plans, I had accepted a reservation for our Bed & Breakfast for the night before my flight. When our guests arrived, they said they needed a quiet place for some study. I asked if they were preparing for an important test. They inquired if I were a Christian and when I responded that I was, they said that they had come to pray and fast, seeking God's direction regarding the possibility of a movie about David, Shepherd boy/King (from the "original script"). One of the men was planning to produce it and the other was considering starring in it. I joined hands with them in prayer, asking that they would find the peace and solitude at the Farm they needed for their quest. They both hugged me and said my initiation of prayer had given them their first confirmation that they were where they were supposed to be! I am not very "savvy" about well-known personalities, and we don't have television, so I was not aware that our actor-guest was quite well-known. I *did* know that he was very handsome and I was grateful that I was a grandmother and could lap up his hugs without wondering, as a young woman might, what impression I was making.

The night before I was to leave, my daughter faxed a message to us. She had additional unsettling medical reports and she was too exhausted to talk about it but wanted us to know. Once again she asked for prayer. I asked our guests to please pray, not only with us, but for us, and I was blessed and calmed by their prayer.

The next morning I awoke at 6:00 a.m. to get ready for the 2-hour drive to the airport. Since I had to leave for my flight early on a day I was supposed to say, "Breakfast Is Served," I came up with a recipe that I could prepare in advance and which Bill could pop into the oven and serve at a more reasonable hour, after I had gone. But as I was getting ready, I realized I really was in need of additional prayer, so I brazenly knocked on our guests' door and asked if they would get up so we could all have breakfast together. They complied and we had a wonderful visit over breakfast, ending with them praying over me for a safe journey--particularly for the drive to the airport, which coincided with the rush hour traffic in Atlanta. Bill asked me to call from the airport to let him know that I had arrived safely, but I was on such a tight schedule I told him I might not have time to call before the flight left. I told him not to worry, and that I'd call him when I arrived in Florida.

I remember driving out of the gate, and then an hour and a half later as the road joined the bottleneck jam on the Interstate, I recall wondering if I was going to make the flight in time. The next thing I knew, I was at the airport *an hour before the time I had allotted as my deadline!* When I called Bill, he was incredulous.

The flight was smooth and we soared over the clouds, but I felt my *spirit* soar when I was able to hug Stephanie and Brandon in person. We had a wonderful two-day visit together and while I was there, I drove over to Jane's house. I brought a big frozen turkey and watermelon to her and said, "It's not that you're a 'turkey,' but turkeys remind me of Thanksgiving and I am thankful for you! And the watermelon is sweet and delightful, and that's what you are. I hope when you use them, you will remember the gratitude in my heart for you."

Upon my return I learned from Bill that one of our B&B guests had been none other than the tall, dark and handsome "Bubba," from "In the Heat of the Night" series. Several friends asked if I'd gotten his autograph, but I didn't even know *who* he was when he was hugging me. I *do* know he's a powerful prayer partner, though! And I also know that the Lord sends people into our lives at times when we are in need. I had been tired and emotionally stretched, and their prayers had lifted me (and the car) above the traffic and into the airport in absolute record-time.

Cowboys and Indians---and Soldiers

In the course of our travels out west, we stopped in a small town in Arizona for lunch one day and did some browsing through the shops nearby. There were some beautifully carved kachina dolls in one of the stores and one in particular really caught my eye. I admired the workmanship and the precision with which it had been fashioned, and kept going back to look at it. Unbeknownst to me at the time, Scott had noticed my interest and tugged on Bill's sleeve. "Mom really likes that carving, Dad."

Bill wasn't quite as impressed with it as I was, and even less impressed at the price. But Scott persisted, "Dad, she doesn't usually like anything as much as she likes that, and your anniversary is next week."

I spoke to the shopkeeper about the carving, and she told me that I might have a chance to meet the artist because he was a Hopi chief and came to town each week on that day to do laundry. As we spoke, she said, "In fact, there is he now, in the old red pick-up truck pulling into the parking lot."

I was thrilled to meet the artist whose hands had fashioned the work of art I had been admiring. He was a man in his late 60's and seemed genuinely pleased that I appreciated his talent.

Bill decided that the carving would be a suitable gift for our anniversary and bought it, and we asked the chief if we could take a photograph of him holding the carving. He said, "No. You and me with kachina." So I ended up with a photograph of me with the artist and his carving.

About two years later I wondered if I could order another carving from him. The first time I wrote to him I sent him a copy of the photo and asked if he remembered me. His response was, "When I first see the letter from Ft. Lauderdale, I think to myself, 'Who the heck I know in Ft. Lauderdale?' But then I see the picture and I rember." He "rembered" lots of things throughout the years, and one year he invited us to attend the Indian ceremonials out on the reservation. We drove for two hours from the nearest town through absolute desolate desert before we arrived at the reservation. We did not pass a single tree during that time, and very little vegetation other than tumbleweed and cactus.

The five of us were among the only non-Indians invited to the ceremonies, and I know that it is an invitation not freely extended. No cameras are allowed on the reservation, and these ceremonials are usually "off-limits" to outsiders. We saw his home and met several members of his family, seven of whom lived in his one-bedroom house.

Over a ten year period I corresponded with the chief and collected three more pieces of his work. I was thrilled to hear that he was invited to an all expense-paid trip to California and honored by an art society for his workmanship, but I wondered how this simple, humble man felt travelling on a jet, being transported from the airport in a taxi, and staying in rather classy accomodations---particularly since the White Man had relegated his people to such a remote outpost.

During our trip to the reservation, our oldest son became interested in Indian history and one of the books he read was about Chief Joseph, whose famous quotation: "I will fight no more forever," became one of Bill Jr.'s favorites. He also enjoyed the movie "Friendly Persuasion," the story of the Quakers and their lives of simple nonviolent coexistence in their culture.

So it was with puzzlement that I received Bill Jr.'s pronouncement that he was going to apply for the Air Force Academy. I told him that I hadn't envisioned raising a son for a militant, warlike career. His response was, "Mom, all your life you've had the freedom to do the things you felt were important." (He was referring to my various battles with city councils, county commissions and other boards). He continued, "And someone else's son has stood behind you throughout the years, safeguarding your freedom to speak your mind. Now it's just my turn. I don't want to kill anyone, and I don't want to be killed, but someone has to stand and be willing to protect that freedom."

I thought of the Indians--who were forced to fight to try to preserve their homeland. I thought about the Quakers--most of whom refused to fight during the Civil War. And I thought about my gangly teenaged son whose commitment to his country was to be willing to lay down his life for it and the freedom it represented. And I prayed that the Lord would guide and direct his steps in the paths of righteousness and justice, and that he would come to recognize that the Lord was the Commander-in-chief over all. While it was not my personal choice that my son follow a military career, I know that the Lord uses different people in different positions to fulfill His plans, and that *ultimately* "the battle belongs to the Lord!"

Like Moses' Response:
"Lead Your People *WHERE?!*"

My son, Bill Jr., was right about my involvement in community matters. For a time, I'm sure the City Council and County Commission thought I was one of multiple clones who appeared simultaneously at meetings across the county. In truth, for a while I did seem to have almost indefatigable energy to see that changes were made to benefit the community. And the Lord provided an aide/friend during those years. After a newspaper article about a road-widening project identified me as a "leader" in the struggle, I received a phone call from a woman named Margaret who asked if she could help in some way. I figured she could help in **any** way, since *I had no idea what I was doing.*

Margaret was a Christian and a strong believer in the power of prayer. We became allied in the premise that the Lord gives strength to those who call upon Him in a united cause.

The County wanted to widen a sleepy little two-lane road (which was bordered by three schools, two ballfields and hundreds of homes with children who had to cross that road regularly) into a major six-lane thoroughfare. All the projections we were able to gather indicated that that particular road would not logically be the best corridor, but we were told the plans could not be stopped.

We thought it would be helpful if our group had a catchy slogan and acronym by which we could be identified, so we became "LIMITT" which stood for Life Is More Important Than Traffic. For over a year and a half we rallied the community to show its opposition to the plan. Finally a compromise plan was instituted, consisting of widening the road to four lanes with a buffer of trees lining the area between the road and the sidewalk.

Almost on the heels of our "success" and my long-awaited "retirement" from municipal involvement, a second cause appeared on the scene. Bordering the road-widening project, there was a 90-acre tract of land that had been an agricultural experiment station, on which the 20-year lease was expiring, and which the owner now wanted to sell. Margaret called me and said she had just uncovered the information and asked if we could reunite to have the land dedicated as parkland. If fighting the road was an uphill battle, then fighting the developers was like climbing Mount Everest---blindfolded! Never had we experienced such opposing power. Many times over the next two years, one of us would become so discouraged that we would want to quit. But never did the Lord allow both of us to become that discouraged at the same time.

We were preparing for an extremely strained City Council meeting and I thought it would be helpful to somehow ease the tension a little. I told Bill, "We've arranged for several people from various groups to speak in behalf of the park proposal: leaders of Boy and Girl Scout troops, Cub Scout dens, youth leaders, etc., and I wonder if you would represent the Indian Guide and Indian Princess programs you are involved in?" Bill said he would. Then I threw in an additional request: "In order to soften the pressure-cooker tension, would you be willing to wear your Indian headband and introduce yourself by the Indian name you use in that group?" His response, was an emphatic, but not unexpected, "Absolutely not!"

The meeting was scheduled for a February 14th. That evening, Bill came home carrying a very large box. My mind was racing. (Lord, don't let that be a *fur* coat that he got from a neighbor who's a fur dealer!) I asked Bill what was in the box and he told me I'd find out later. After dinner, he put the box in the car and off we went.

I was right about anticipating a difficult meeting; tempers were flaring and the atmosphere was dark indeed. After several people had spoken, I leaned over and told Bill he should be prepared to speak next, and he left the Council chambers, saying he'd be right back. And in a minute he was back, decked-out in a full medicine-man headdress that reached to his waist! (*That's* what was in that big box.) I was shocked! The members of the Council were shocked! When Bill reached the podium he said, "How! Me Chief Thundercloud, and me member of Indian Guide and Indian Princess program. Me here to speak for them." I think that's probably all he said----at least that's all anyone heard---because the entire Council broke up into uncontrolled laughter. That was the pressure valve that served to release pent-up emotions, and became the turning point of the meeting so that rational discussion could begin. One of the Councilmen said it brought back memories of his own days in the Indian Guides program and the fun he had with his children, and that he could understand how beneficial a large passive park could be for the youth of the community.

We won at the city level that day, receiving a commitment that the city would pledge 1/4 of the purchase price *if* the county would pay the balance. And Bill won kudos from me for stepping into a role I knew was hard for him. (Imagine how hard it is for a prim-and-proper man to be married to someone like me, who's always requesting that he stretch his horizons beyond the limits!)

We still had the County Commission hurdle to cross, however. At the meeting there, I realized as I was delivering my carefully prepared remarks and facts, *not one* of the commissioners was listening! I was frustrated; I stopped reading my statement and accused them of the travesty of a pretend show of public input when they weren't interested in listening to facts anyway! The vote that day was against the park, 4-3.

Following the meeting I saw one of the commissioners in the hall and angrily expressed my frustration at the attitude of the commissioners. He asked me to follow him to his office, where he gave me a poem entitled "Don't Quit." He said if I felt so strongly about my cause that I shouldn't give up. And _he_ had been one of the votes *against* us just minutes before! Now I was really angry, and I told him it was very difficult to keep rallying the forces time after time, when in reality the Commission was going to steamroll right over public opinion and the good of the community. I thought he had some nerve to tell me to keep on keeping-on, when he was clearly not on our side. What a perverse sense of humor that was!

Nevertheless, I took that poem home and reread it. And if nothing else, it reiterated to me the importance of not giving up. The

Bible doesn't tell us to run for a while; it says to *persevere to the end.* So Margaret and I went before the Lord, sought strength and courage, and went on for several more rounds. Then in a move that surprised us (and perhaps other members of the Commission), the commissioner who had given me the poem was the "swing-vote" the next time the matter came up for discussion, pushing the vote over the edge in favor of the park!

We were advised that even after the land was acquired, the real stumbling block would be receiving funding to develop it into a park. Margaret's expertise was research, and she discovered that there were funds available through the Department of Natural Resources. Usually, even for favorable projects, they only granted about 1/3 of the amount requested, so it was suggested we ask for three times what we hoped to receive. In our presentation, we filled the portfolio with all the newspaper articles the park issue had generated, and pointed out the strong community support involved. We requested a million dollars. (Why not?! Does not our God own all the cattle on a thousand hills?) Nevertheless, no one was more surprised than we, when the DNR granted $900,000 for this project! We were told that was an unprecedented ratio.

The ultimate outcome therefore was Victory: victory in the Lord, and praise and thanksgiving for the beautiful, peaceful, passive park that graces a community that needed a park, not 250 additional houses. My heart soars whenever I see the people walking, jogging, pushing baby strollers, picnicking, playing "catch" with children, riding the pedal-boats, fishing, feeding the ducks, or just stretched out and relaxing on the grass in that beautiful tree-shaded park.

P.S. Those 250 additional houses would have necessitated the requirement for a six-lane road, but the park negated it. And the Lord didn't tell us about the park until we had gone the distance on the road-widening scenario. *For sure, I wouldn't have signed up for that interminable 3-1/2 year stint!* Like He did with Moses, He didn't reveal His plan all at one time. He just said, "Lead my people." Wouldn't Moses have bolted if he'd known about the Red Sea, the forty years in the desert, and the grumblings? Best we don't know the whole plan; one day at a time is sufficient for us mere mortals. Leave the long-range planning to the Master Planner.

P.P.S. After some discussion, the County decided to name the park "Heritage Park." After initially writing this story, I decided to look up what the Bible had to say on the subject of "heritage," and felt a Cheshire-cat smile cross my lips as I read Exodus 6:7-8 and Psalm 135:12, paraphrased in my own words as:

> "I will take you as my own people, and you shall have me as your God. You will know that I, the Lord, am your God when I free you from the (City and County's intentions) and bring you into the **land** which I swore to give to (Arlene and Margaret)."

and

> "**And he made their land a heritage**, the heritage of (Arlene and Margaret) his people."

All Things Are Possible
Through God Who Strengthens Me!

In my youth, I remember being impressed by certain outstanding feats of accomplishment that people throughout history had achieved. I read biographies about people with disabilities, like Hellen Keller, Joni Erickson and Franklin Roosevelt. In particular, I liked to read inspirational stories about those who had been the "First to . . . " --such as the first to discover electricity, the first pilot, the first to conquer _(fill in the blank)_. I contemplated the thrill it would have been to be one of those or even to *know* one of them.

As I think back to how I had raised my own children, I am ashamed to admit that I had never suggested they stretch their sights to achieve difficult goals. In fact, when Christy came home from school one day at age 10 and asked if she could take violin lessons, initially I tried to dissuade her, saying that no one in our family was musically inclined, and we couldn't help on an instrument as difficult as a violin. And when Scott wanted to do a science fair project that seemed rather ambitious for a 12-year-old, I told him it appeared he had taken on an awfully large endeavor. Scott also thought he might try for an Eagle Scout award and had a difficult project he wanted to get permission from the county to do. I told him that dealing with governmental agencies was really an uphill battle and suggested he think of a less complicated project. When Billy wanted to jog with a neighbor so he could attempt a marathon at the age of 13, I said it was much too far, and besides it might be hard on his growing body. And when he later said he had his heart set on a service academy, I explained that so few who applied were accepted, and I encouraged him to have an alternate plan.

Never in my wildest imagination did I ever think I would meet a person who had performed at Carnegie Hall---that revered and hallowed hall that had been the site of so many renowned debuts. But in 1988 I flew up to New York City to sit in a boxseat at Carnegie Hall and listen to a concert by a youth orchestra, one of whose violinists I personally knew. With my heart beating rapidly and tears of wonder blurring my vision, I savored the experience as one of the highlights of my life. I couldn't believe that the Lord had fulfilled one of my unspoken dreams!

Years later I attended a very moving and impressive Eagle Scout ceremony at which the town's mayor and a county commissioner, among others, extolled both the merits of the project that had been accomplished and the personal attributes of the young man receiving the coveted award. I knew that recipient, and I felt proud to be in attendance as he received his just reward for completing a worthy public service. I realized that the Lord had indeed allowed me to see the second of my fantasies. Since I was aware that the Eagle Scout had previously won awards at the County and State levels with intricate science fair projects, it doubled my sense of satisfaction! It seemed as though my cup had runneth over.

Then I was granted the privilege of an invitation to the graduation ceremonies at the Air Force Academy in Colorado Springs as a special young man was being commissioned as an officer. I also recalled that years earlier I had stood on the sidelines as this lad had completed a marathon. I was startled to realize that all the seemingly unreachable desires of my heart had been fulfilled!

It is with humility and contrition that I confess that I was wrong not to believe in my children's dreams. Nevertheless, even without my *initial* advocacy, they often countermanded my humble opinion and stepped out to stretch their horizons. (After they had embarked on a project, I did muster up the ability to be a cheerleader, however.) And they are the ones I saw perform at Carnegie Hall, accept an Eagle Scout award, win State science fair trophies, run marathons, and be commissioned at the Air Force Academy!

It just goes to prove that the Lord has created each of us special and unique, and if we follow the small still voice within us, we are capable of attaining the unattainable (humanly speaking, because *all things are possible with God!*)

You Shall Renew Your Strength and Soar . . .

As I reflect back on the first 26-mile marathon that 13-year old Bill Jr. participated in, I remember afresh my uneasiness and anxiety. Even by South Florida standards, it was a cold 45° January day, and I thought a 26-mile run was too far for anyone---much less my "child,"--- to engage in.

Bill and Billy drove down to the Orange Bowl, the starting point, before dawn. My mother, the other children and I were stationed at various spots along the route to offer moral support. Scott and I were at the 22-mile mark, and after what seemed like a million joggers had passed us, there were only "stragglers" left. These approached at a snail's pace and were in visibly poor condition. Then, in the distance, bobbing up and down and not appearing to be moving forward with any momentum at all, I spied a familiar figure. "Scott, is that *Billy*?" I asked. He said it looked like him.

It took a full five minutes for him to actually approach us, and I noted that he had shed his warm-up jacket. (When the race began, he convinced Bill he wouldn't need it because he'd "work up a sweat" in a few minutes, and Bill had believed him!) His skin was sort of blue, and he looked as if he didn't have enough energy to pick up his foot one more time to place it in front of him. I asked if he'd like a jacket, he said he would, and I quickly enfolded him in a spare one I had. (It may have been a sweatshirt, but its fleece was appropriate for the little lost lamb he looked like.) I told him that even if he quit at the 22-mile mark, he had already performed a tremendous feat, and could be proud of what he had accomplished. He adamantly said he wasn't quitting.

That meant I had to switch gears from helping him drop out gracefully, to helping him regain his confidence so he could finish. *My* desire was that he'd stop, but I felt duty-bound to cheerlead for him if his dream was to keep on. I changed my tack to, "Well, then you *can* make it! You've gone almost the whole way and you only have a couple more miles to go." All the time we were talking, I was *walking backwards* faster than he was jogging forward, if that helps describe just how exhausted he was. I peeled an orange and gave it to him, assuring him we'd go ahead and meet him at the finish line.

My prayer was, "Lord, they only give out official print-outs for those runners who complete the marathon in five hours or less, so please let him make the time so he'll always have *tangible* evidence that he completed this race." Scott and I drove back to the Orange Bowl and waited inside the stadium. The clock was ticking off the time of the race and, as it got within twelve minutes of the cut-off time, I was getting concerned. Scott and I wnt back outside the Bowl and saw about a dozen stragglers dragging in, and then---suddenly, like Mercury---came a mighty runner, passing all the stragglers and coming in like greased lightning. It was my boy! I was astounded that he had been re-energized and was able to finish like a "winner." He received his official print-out! (The following year he was able to shave nearly an hour and a half off his time!)

Five years later when he went to the U.S. Air Force Academy, he had the stamina and vigor to withstand the trials and hardships he had to face. He says that USAFA is pronounced U-Suffa, because that's what you do there. And although there is a more than 25% attrition rate among students who drop out within the unrelentlessly trying first six months, I believe he received his "Basic Training" when he was a 13-year old who simply would not quit.

At the end of a rigorous four years, he earned the right to wear an Academy graduation ring, on which he had inscribed the reference "Isaiah 40:31." I know the meaning contained in the words was very near to his heart, and when he told me about the inscription I thought back to that cold January day and the marathon that was such a turning point in his life. It was also the Lord's ongoing lesson to me that it is with the *Lord's* strength, and not our own, that we are able to do that which seems impossible.

The inscription on his ring referred to the same words the Lord wanted to inscribe on my heart: "They that *hope in the Lord* will renew their strength, they will soar as with eagles' wings; they shall run and not get weary, walk and not grow faint."

Rain, Rain, Go Away . . .
Come Again Another Day

As I contemplate the fact that my high school class celebrated its fortieth reunion a couple of years back, I find myself reflecting that must surely be a "misprint," and that it was just our fourteenth! I mean, after all, I'm not even thirty yet, am I? And who are those little children who keep calling me "gran'ma"?

But then reality kicks back in, and I admit that the numbers don't lie (nor do the wrinkles). What is most incredible is that several of my high school "buddies"---(that's what we were back then; now we're more like biddies)---are even better friends now after all those years! In fact, while we went to school in South Florida, three of us now have homes in the North Georgia mountains, within a half-hour's drive of one another. And it was not a concerted effort on our parts to achieve that...it just sort of "happened," unbeknownst to each of us. The best part is that now our relationship is grounded in the Lord, and is deeper and more meaningful than when we were just a bunch of giggly teens.

A couple of years back, my friend Sharon called to ask if I could go on a hike before she had to go back to Miami. We made our plans to hike Raven's Cliff Falls, but that morning loomed gray and drizzly. I called Sharon and said, "It's raining here." She replied, "It's raining here, too, but I have raingear. Are you game?" I was "game," but I didn't know *HOW* game I was going to be called upon to be that day!

We met halfway, left one car behind and travelled toward Raven's Cliff. The name of the Falls indicates a brief idea of the type of hike that lay ahead. We strapped on our backpacks with lunches packed, put our ponchos over our packs, picked up our walking sticks and started out. Even in the light drizzle it is a beautiful place to be, and for much of the walk the trail runs beside a beautiful creek. It is the kind of trail that is narrow, with gnarled roots and rocks to manuever around---a singlefile type of trail that is

2.5 miles long, with the last half-mile quite steep and bringing into view a waterfall that runs through a massive rock.

After we had been walking for about an hour, it was no longer drizzling. The rain was now torrential. The trail had turned to pure red Georgia clay, which was oozing up around our shoes and making the trail quite slippery. I called to Sharon, "You know, there's nothing that says we HAVE to do this trail today. Maybe we could reschedule it for another time. What do you think?" She agreed and we started back toward the car. She asked, "Are you hungry?" Actually, though I was quite hungry, I replied, "Yes, but it's nearly an hour back to the car." Sharon reminded me that we had our lunch with us and she said, "How much wetter can we get?"

So we sat down on a huge icy-cold rock at the edge of the creek and proceeded to have a "picnic." (There were no ants!) As we sat there with the rain dripping off our rain hats onto our sandwiches, I imagined what we would look like if anyone could see us. I said, "Did you ever think--when we were in high school--that one day we'd be sitting together in the middle of the woods, on a cold rock, eating lunch in a monsoon?!" We got a fit of laughing and I nearly lost my breath. I said, "I can just see it now. If I lose my breath and die, the coroner will have to list my cause of death as 'Death by choking while laughing during a picnic in the woods during a rainstorm'." P. S. The sandwiches were delicious, and she was right: how much wetter *could* we get?

When we finished eating, we resumed our walk to the car, loudly singing an old hiking song, "Val-der-eeeeeeee, val-der-raaaahhhhh . . ." as we approached the parking lot. There is a steep embankment from the trail up to the pavement, and we couldn't see that there was another vehicle parked up there as we came over the bank. We were still singing and laughing---and then we saw them: three forest rangers sitting in a truck next to Sharon's Florida-licensed car. They must have wondered if the crazy "flat-landers" (as Floridans are called by folks in the mountains) still on that trail in the storm might be in need of help. They looked mighty surprised at the bedraggled grandmothers who appeared before them! "Good hike, ladies?" one of them asked. "Oh, yes," we replied, "it was wonderful!"

Actually, it may not have been "wonderful," but it was certainly "wonder-filled"! Whenever I recall memorable moments, I always think back to that day--and other similar days when things did not go "as planned," but when I was given an opportunity to share the Lord's bounty (both visually and food-wise) with a friend who was obviously one of His gifts to me. I remember a hike with Tommy one day up at Brasstown Bald, when she and I stopped to eat our lunch and I said, "Tommy, isn't this the most perfect day we have ever hiked? There's a cool breeze blowing and not a bug in sight." Instantly there was a clap of thunder and, before we had finished our lunch, *huge* drops of rain began to fall. She urged me to hurry and get the raingear out. Within minutes the mountain was ablaze with lightning flashes and the rain came down in buckets! Even with our hastily donned raingear, by the time we slip-slided down the muddy banks to our car at the base of the mountain, we were pretty dirty. It is reassuring to know that even in such visibly soiled circumstances, through the blood of the Lamb, the Lord sees us as white as snow. But I think He must be laughing, too!

God Is the Potter; I Am the Clay, Hooray!

I am grateful that God is the Potter and I am merely the clay. I remember once hearing that each person is created to be a special work of art in the hands of the Master Artisan. Whether we are clay or marble, the Artist will fashion us. If we are clay, we are more easily molded, but if we are rigid and unbending marble, it takes a lot of striking of the mallet to change us. Nevertheless, both become finished pieces in the Hands of the Master. As for me, I continuously have to learn that being marble is much less pleasant than being clay!

Nevertheless, even clay goes through a rather grueling set of circumstances before becoming the finished work it is meant to be. It must first be kneaded, watered, spun on the potter's wheel, pounded and then---horrors!---put into the fire. If the clay could talk, I'm sure it would complain that the artist's intentions seemed to be to *destroy it* by pounding, drowning, spinning or fire! However, all these steps are necessary if the finished piece is to endure.

And I am infinitely more grateful that He is God and I am not! So many of the situations and circumstances that the Lord has led me through have included some poundings, some drownings, some times when I felt like I was spinning out-of-control, and some seasons in the fire, but the final product is always quite awesome in the hands of an awesome God.

For example, this book would never have been written had I but known that's what I was doing when I started. I would have argued and debated that I couldn't "be" an author. But the Master Artisan never asks us what we think we could do or be. . . He just uses us to do and be what He---in His infinite wisdom---*enables* us to do and be!

Consider Thomas Edison, Benjamin Franklin, Henry Ford, Billy Graham, Abraham Lincoln, Michelangelo, Mother Teresa, or the Wright brothers. Each of them began life as a rather ordinary child in rather ordinary circumstances. Imagine what a different world this would have been if they had been constrained by an unwillingness to step out and do what had never been done before (or in the case of Lincoln, Graham, Michelangelo and Mother Teresa, what had never been done on the *scope* of what they were ultimately to accomplish). Do you think any of them initially had even an <u>inkling</u> of the impact their "ordinary" lives would have on the world and its history? I rather doubt it.

Doesn't it give you pause to wonder what the Lord can do with your "ordinary" life if only you are willing to surrender it to His use? You might never go down in the history books (nor shall I), but the Lord uses ordinary people to do extraordinary things in the unseen realm of His plan. And His plan is always so much larger and more grand than anything we could envision.

So next time you get a "silly" idea that seems to come from out-side yourself, and which you think you are too ordinary to pursue, step out in faith and follow the leading you perceive. It may be something as simple as picking up the phone or notepaper to reach out to someone you don't know very well (maybe your Senator or perhaps the principal of your child's school) and tell them you felt led to pray for them. Or maybe it's delivering a homemade meal for the widow who lives down the street. That seems like an incongruous idea, doesn't it? Why would you be called to do such a thing? Well, it just may be that the Lord needs to reach out to that person in a way that doesn't make sense to you. . .but then again, He is the Potter, and we are merely the clay, and since when does the clay question the Potter???!

In the same way that an artist perceives the finished product long before it is completed, the Lord has a long-range view of situations. We are limited to short-sightedness and rather limited vision. But if you've ever been on the receiving end of someone's comment like, "I can't believe you called today; I <u>so</u> needed that encouragement!" then you know the joy of being touched by the hands of One who is the ultimate Master Artist!

Did You Say Follow or Fallow, Lord?

The Lord puts different people in our lives for different purposes. Some are to instruct us, some are to lead us, some bring us comfort, some encourage us, some are for us to instruct, lead, comfort or encourage, and some seem to have no other purpose than strictly for fun! Lucia definitely belongs in the latter category for me. No matter when the two of us get together (and this has been true for nearly thirty years), we manage to do the zaniest things imaginable! You would think time would bring maturity in this regard, but not for us! There is a certain chemisty between us that makes us giggle like children when we are together. Lucia told me that I am the only friend whose house she goes to, where she feels comfortable taking her shoes off, stretching out on the floor and totally relaxing while we visit.

We first met when we lived next door to one another in an apartment complex in Ft. Lauderdale. Lucia had a two-month old baby; I had a 1 1/2-year old and was pregnant with a second child. During a power black-out one night, we and our husbands found ourselves on our adjoining porches sharing candles, snacks, cold drinks and fellowship, and friendship blossomed.

The funniest incident was the time we went to the mall with our children, who at that time were my 3-year old, her 2-year old, my 1-year old (all of whom were in one stroller), and her six-week old baby whom she was carrying in her arms. Oh, and I should mention that I was also pregnant (actually for a few years it seemed like I was always pregnant). Lucia saw a dress in a shop window and asked if I'd hold the baby and watch the children while she dashed in to try it on. I strolled up and down the mall for a few minutes and when she came out of the store, I said, "Do you want to see something funny? Walk about two paces behind me and watch the expressions on peoples' faces as they see me with the three children in the stroller, an infant in my arms, and then they notice that I am pregnant!"

One night while our husbands were at home with the children, both Lucia and I dashed off to do some grocery shopping. Since the store was closing in about fifteen minutes, we were moving at a fast clip. I had left my purse in my shopping cart , but as I went to put some items in my cart I noticed that my purse was gone. I shouted to Lucia and, still pushing our carts wildly through the aisles, we went in different directions looking for the person who had taken my purse. A couple of minutes later we met in the center of the store and I was distraught to learn that neither of us had any luck. Suddenly I glanced in Lucia's cart and was shocked to see my purse! She had been racing all over the store looking for the thief, when in fact *she had taken my entire cart with my purse in it* --- and I had her cart! I know the weary storekeepers wished we'd do our laughing outside so they could close the store, but it took us awhile to compose ourselves sufficiently to make our way to the check-out counter.

Lucia is the kind of friend who can candidly offer constructive criticism, and she is one whose opinion I sought when I started writing these stories. Her help was invaluable, and she was also a source of encouragement. Although Lucia and I had been on different spiritual wavelengths for many years, she said she was touched by the tales of how the Lord had worked through me to reach out to others. I was also aware that for about a year or so prior to my requests for editing services, Lucia had seemed to be seeking---and finding---the Lord's calling in her own life.

Taking that into consideration, I wanted to be careful not to jeopardize either our friendship or her spiritual growth by "coming on too strong" regarding the Lord. Nevertheless, one day I found myself confronting her about an issue I thought she needed to deal with. I asked if she had ever been able to forgive her ex-husband. He had done some terrible things and she was quite adamant that she wasn't going to forgive him and didn't think he "deserved" to be forgiven. I continued with a persistence that seemed to cross the line of comfortability---for both of us. I tried to let go of the matter, but found myself being insistent. Our visit ended with my asking her to at least think about it.

The next day was a Sunday, and that afternoon we met again rather unexpectedly. Lucia was quite anxious to tell me, incredulously, that the sermon at her church had been on the *very* subject I had been speaking to her about---including the offenses that her ex-husband had been involved in! She told me she felt an overwhelming conviction that the Lord was dealing with her in a powerful way. She said she realized that He had used me to *fallow* the garden of her soul in readiness for the message He had meant for her to hear. Her words were, "I've read your stories of how God used you in the lives of others, but when it actually *touched my life personally*, it was mind-boggling!"

Afterwards I looked up the word "fallow" in my dictionary and discovered that it means "the tilling of land without sowing it for a season; to plow, harrow and break up land without seeding; to destroy weeds and insects, and *render it mellow.*"

This revelation cleared up a lot of questions in my mind about why I had been called to do what I had considered unpleasant tasks. I had always envisioned myself in the role of a seed-sower---a kind of female-counterpart to Johnny Appleseed, dropping seeds of great worth as I walked along the pathway of life---but now I could see that I had often been used in the distasteful role of one who upsets the apple cart. I wanted people to like me, and one who confronts is often seen as intrusive. However, I saw that the Lord had pressed me into service in difficult situations to confront people who were in need of having their hearts "broken up, plowed, and rendered mellow," so that He could continue with the steps of seeding, watering, fertilizing and shining the sun (Son?) on. Whew! It was an incredible revelation! Lord, is that what you used me to do? I've always wanted to be Your follower, Lord . . . and if You want, I'll be Your fallower, too!

The Lost-and-Found Department

There seem to be so many books, movies and television shows about self-determining incidents lately. Most of them seem to extol the virtues of Positive Thinking or Power Thinking, and the stories appear to reinforce the theory that we are in charge of our own destiny. And they are related to give a hurting world "Hope."

Something about that premise is disturbing. It is like a nagging memory of something which comes back to raise its ugly head over and over again. It has an aura about it that assumes that we live in a universe without a God who has created us, wants to have relationship with us, and to whom we are responsible.

It's like a remake of the story of the Garden of Eden, only with a 20th Century twist. Instead of eating of the tree of good and evil so that they would have all knowledge and be like God themselves, today's Adam and Eve would only have to embrace one of three theories: 1) that God doesn't exist, 2) that everything *is* God and we ourselves are God, or 3) we can attain the goal of "becoming" God, either in this life or by coming back multiple times.

In the permissive and irresponsible atmosphere that prevails these days, it is easy to see how people would believe one of the three theories. It is not in our nature to voluntarily choose to be subject to anyone else's authority. Why, even from earliest infancy a baby makes his wants known---rather vociferously, in fact! One of his first words is "No," after which he learns how to use punctuation and how to put an exclamation mark after his pronouncement. And unless that child is carefully "trained in the way he should go" and later voluntarily accepts that path for himself, he remains an unbridled "free spirit" who believes that his rights are paramount over everyone else's, and he is accountable to no one but himself.

As for me, I know Who created me, and He knows me---and while He loves me immeasurably, I am accountable to Him. In times when His ways are not clear, I seek clarity and He shows me the way; if it is a difficult path, He gives me strength, sustenance, courage and comfort on the journey. I wish I were "perfect" and obedient at all times, but I am not, so I am grateful that He is infinitely patient with me and quick to forgive when I turn to Him after falling short of the mark. He not only *allows* U-turns, He encourages them!

What I find most disturbing is how easily even a committed Christian---who knows the Lord and follows Him---can be distracted from His way and led down a path that *seems* to be in line with His teachings but which is in fact far afield. I've learned that the enemy doesn't have to cause me to do an about-face, he only has to get me distracted from the Lord and headed <u>slightly</u> off the mark. Soon I find myself on a path seemingly "parallel" to the Lord's, but with a chasm between us, and the destination suddenly different.

I saw a graphic vision of this chasm recently when the youth group from my Ft. Lauderdale church returned from a statewide youth rally called "Acquire the Fire," in which over 12,000 teens participated. One of the chaperone-moms kept hearing the repeated phrase "Generation X" as a description of what society calls our young people today. She asked one of the youth leaders what that meant, and he told her it means they are a "Lost Generation." When the youth returned from the rally, they were renewed, refreshed and re-committed---"on fire" for the Lord. As they were relating their testimonies, I suddenly saw that while they had gone to the rally slightly akilter, as Generation X, (many admitted they had back-slidden away from they Lord), they returned somewhat altered, as Generation ✝ ... "Found and Restored." Jesus said He came *to seek the Lost*! And by the power of His cross he had righted their paths: from ✘ ...to ..✘ ... to ✝ . It was a simple operation, but it required <u>open-heart</u> surgery. Many of them admitted that they had gone to the rally reluctantly---at the insistence or urging of their parents. Nevertheless, the Lord knows His own, and He seeks them out and carries them home gently in His arms.

Months after the youth from my Ft. Lauderdale church returned "on fire," and the Lord gave me the vision of "X = Lost," the teens from my Georgia church went to a youth rally and also came back renewed and restored. Ironically, the theme T-shirt for

182

their weekend was **X**-treme, meaning that the Christian life required an extreme lifestyle and commitment. And one of the girls told us that during the week there was an assignment to "re-write" 1 Corinthians into an updated understanding for these modern times. She wrote hers from the vantage point of a teen, and when she read her composition at church, there was hardly a dry eye in the congregation. It is with the permission of the author that it is shared here:

I Corinthians 13
Paraphrased from a Teenager's Point of View

If I say all the cool sayings and sing all the cool songs, but do not love the people I speak to, I am only making an empty noise..

If I donate all my leopard skin clothes and platform shoes but do not love the receiver, then I have given nothing but thread and leather.

Love waits on the date God wants it to have and doesn't become smart-mouthed when its parents say, No."

Love doesn't get mad at the insulting comment made by its best friend, and Love won't remember that comment either.

Love doesn't enjoy being at the party it knows it shouldn't be at and is happy to share why it wasn't heart-broken that it wasn't invited.

Love is willing to be the designated driver and doesn't run tell everyone who it drove for.

Love always hopes its friends will stop doing drugs, but doesn't desert them if they don't.

When psychics are wrong, trends are out of style, and <u>Seventeen</u> magazine gives bad advice, Love won't fail.

Since we are teenagers, we talk like teenagers, think like teenagers and reason like teenagers, but the thing that makes us different is that we are Christian teenagers.

And now these three remain---boyfriends, clothes and Love, but the only one of these that even matters is Love.

Katie Rybka
Centrifuge, August, 1997

Note: When Katie gave me the copy of this inspiring and inspired message, she said, ". . .but really, it wasn't me. God gave me the words. I could not have thought of it on my own." (hmmmm, that sounds sort of familiar.)

"**X**" kept cropping up over and over during the time I was writing this book. My friend Tammy from Blairsville and I both felt led to start writing a book about the same time. We encouraged each other regularly and whenever one of us would get a rejection slip from a publisher, we would be sure to call the other with our one-upmanship news that we now had one more rejection than the other one had! When I told Tammy about the X Generation and the X-treme T-shirts, she told me another and very moving story about her own impact with an "X." And that, with the permission of the author of Angel Feathers, (which will probably be in print about the same time as this book) is also reprinted here.

LESSONS FROM A HOMELESS CAT

...You are not your own; you were bought at a price. (1Cor. 6:19-20)

I can honestly say I've learned as much about the grace of God in my local animal shelter as I have learned in church.

When my beloved family cat wandered away and never returned home, I drove to the animal shelter to buy myself another one. The newspaper had printed a picture of a beautiful white cat living at the shelter, and I wanted her badly. I phoned ahead and told the manager I would be there to pick her up shortly. Much to my chagrin, however, they allowed her to be adopted by another woman just as I was turning into the parking lot. "Sorry, lady," they told me, "'First come, first served' is our policy."

An employee sensed my disappointment and suggested that I look around to find another cat to love. There were so many

184

homeless cats and kittens peering out of their cages at me I thought my heart would break.

I prayed a quick prayer that God would direct me to the aminal I should choose. Soon my attention was drawn to a half-grown, long-haired calico cat. She began yowling mournfully when I stopped at her cage. She had the potential of becoming a beautiful animal, but looked so frail and forlorn huddled in the corner of that cold, steel cage. My heart was so moved by her pathetic cry I knew I could never leave her there. I told the manager, "I'll take *her!*" I paid the thirty-dollar adoption fee and filled out the necessary paperwork. In her file I read that the cat's previous owner had called her "Cleo."

As I walked back over to her cage I noticed an index card with a big black "X" taped to the bars. "What does this mean?" I asked, pointing to the card. The manager replied, "Ma'am, this cat was left here six weeks ago. That 'X' means she was the next animal to be put to sleep. You just saved her life!"

I released the latch and opened the door, but the cat huddled in fear against the back of the cage. "Here, kitty, kitty," I called. I reached inside to pull her to me and said, "Come on, kitty. You don't have to live here anymore. *You* are *mine...I bought* you!"

As I said those words I felt the spirit of God descend upon me, and in my head I heard these words, "Tammy, *you* are *mine*. I have bought you with a price, the blood of my Son. This cat did nothing to make you choose her to be part of your family, just as you did nothing to make Me love and choose you. Just as you adopted this helpless animal, so have I looked at *you* in pity and compassion and made you *My* child. This is grace."

Sometimes God speaks and teaches us valuable spiritual lessons in the most unlikely places. Chills ran up my arms as I stood looking at that skinny cat timidly hunched beneath the card that pronounced her worthy of death. I thought of all of us who have been blinded by Satan, the father of lies. He makes us feel rejected, defeated, unloved and unwanted, until we find ourselves in the same situation as that poor cat--miserable and forgotten. Just like that animal, we have sat in our squalor and hopelessness day after day, month after month and year after year, just trying to survive, never daring to dream that we could be free.

We are created in the image of God--most precious and holy creations, wonderfully made to reflect His workmanship and glory. When Satan's work is completed, we, the fallen children of the Most High, stand stained, disgraced and ashamed before our Creator. We live and move, but have no being.

Just as Cleo's fate was sealed with that "X," I envisioned Satan with a thick marker gleefully marking us with ugly black "X's." For every sin, every mistake, every failure, "X . . .X . . . X . . .X!" I imagined him laughing as he stands before Jesus pointing his accusing finger at the miserable multitudes of wretched people ruined by sin as he pronounces us worthy of death.

But then, just like when that cat began yowling at me, I imagined a most beautiful sound beginning to rise before the throne of God . . . the unmistakable sweet sound of a sinner crying out for mercy. Jesus cannot help but be moved with compassion when those enslaved in sin's bondage cry out to him, "Lord, save me!"

I pictured Jesus walking the roads of hell unlocking prison doors, breaking our chains, and setting us free. "You don't have to live like this anymore. Come and go with me," I could hear Him say. "You are mine...I bought you with my blood."

When I paid for my cat I got a receipt. If Satan rushes against us to make a second claim after we have been adopted into God's family, all we have to do is call for Jesus. Standing there before Satan, He will open and present His nail-scarred palms, His eternal, indisputable proof-of-purchase. "Paid in Full," written in red!

When I got home I changed Cleo's name to "Xena," which means "princess." I took that dreadful "X" on her cage and made something beautiful out of it, just as God takes our sin and ugliness and works it for our good so that we might be declared righteous and worthy. The Bible promises that as children of God we will also have new names when we get to heaven. As children of King Jesus, we will be princes and princesses in His glorious kingdom! The former life will have passed away, and all things will be new!

Aah, amazing grace, how sweet the sound, that saved a homeless cat----and somebody like me.

by Tammy M. Floyd

I don't think it is a coincidence that the "X" keeps cropping up and that it is a powerful and visual symbol of the kind of changed life the Lord has in mind for us. I think you will agree that the three stories above were X-citing, X-traordinary and X-cellent! And it is no coincidence that the Greek symbol for Christ is "X." Christ, the life-changer . . .

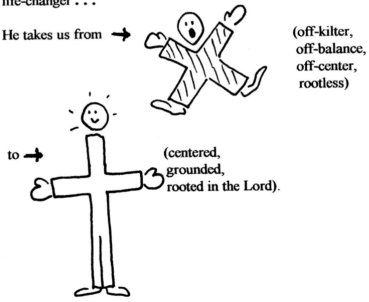

He takes us from ➔ (off-kilter, off-balance, off-center, rootless)

to ➔ (centered, grounded, rooted in the Lord).

A Sturdy Tree Must Have Deep Roots

In order to survive the storms of life, a tree must be firmly rooted. The same is true of a human. And I have found it to be infinitely true in my own life.

The Lord provides soil, water and sunlight so that a tree may grow tall and strong. In the case of humans, those elements equate to family, friends and the light of the Son.

My extended family includes dozens of cousins, lots of aunts and uncles, and various and sundry second cousins and relatives-in-law, as well as a wealth of others to whom I am related through being members of the family of God.

There is, in particular, a group of cousins who have always been supportive and encouraging throughout the years, and upon whom I can count to bring along laughter and joy when they come. They've been willing to entrust to me the responsibility for planning family reunions and celebrations, and always seem to think that the plans are "perfect." (Have you ever been in charge of making those kinds of arrangements and had the attendees complain that it should have been different . . .either in another place, or at another time, or for less cost, or in a more attractive setting, etc.? It sort of takes the wind out of the planner's sails). But this group is lavish in their appreciation and generous with their gratitude.

The times I rented the caboose on the Smoky Mountain Railroad for eighteen of us, or reserved six cabins at a lakefront resort for thirty-two of us---(where young Scott was dunked in the lake and then rolled in the sand for a Shake-and-Bake experience)---provided lasting happy memories that we all still remember with nostalgia. We especially remember the thrilling waterslide that challenged our definition of "fear." Each person went home with a notebook filled with lovenotes from the other attendees, affirming what they enjoyed most about the notebook-owner. Those were times to build onto the foundation that the Lord had provided, and helped strengthen family roots---the ties that bind.

Recently a friend told me she had visited Charleston, SC and noticed that all the Spanish moss was missing from the big old oak trees, a casualty of the last hurricane. Upon reflection, I realized that moss is simply a parasite---something the dictionary characterizes as a "free-loader, leech, bloodsucker, hanger-on." In time of trial, such as a hurricane, the moss was simply blown away. The oaks, on the other hand, because they are firmly grounded and deeply rooted, weathed the storm's fury and remained standing.

It made me reflect that people are like either the oak or the moss. We've all encountered those who seem to weather the storms of life in much different fashion than others. Some seem to have a deep root-system and stand firm despite the turmoil, while others seem to be blown to and fro by any strong breeze that comes along.

Jeremiah 17 contains an encouragement on this subject. "Blessed is the man who trusts in the Lord, whose confidence is in Him. He will be like a tree planted by the water that sends out its roots by the stream. It does not fear when heat comes; its leaves are always green. It has no worries in a year of drought and never fails to bear fruit." What a promise, and all we have to do in order to receive the blessing is *trust in the Lord*.

Caterpillars Into Butterflies

During the time we were involved with extensive home remodeling many years ago, we were dealing with a number of situations simultaneously. Since the renovations included the kitchen, our refrigerator was in the front hallway and the microwave was in the entryway. In addition, a pregnant girl was living with us and the children's bedrooms had been disrupted in order to accomodate our guest.

In the midst of all this chaos, one day the foreman came to me and said, "We have to make a decision on the placement of windows. Can you come with me for a few minutes?" Just an instant prior to his question, I had felt a very strong impulse directing me to "Go to the typewriter." I know I looked as bewildered as he did when I hesitatingly said, "Uhhh. . . can you wait a minute. I have to go to the typewriter first."

As I sat down and placed my fingers on the keys, a torrent of words poured out, and in about five minutes I had covered an entire page with typing. It was about butterflies---and more! As I took it out of the typewriter, I said to the foreman, "Oh, my! Read this!" As he read it, he began crying, and I said, "Oh, was it meant for *you*? I thought it was for the pregnant girl who is staying with us." It opened the door to a deep discussion involving his relationship with one of his daughters.

Through the years I would share a copy of it with people who seemed to need it, and from time to time I would hear that someone had read it on a bulletin board where they worked or seen it in a Marriage Encounter newsletter, etc. That little story was getting around on wings of its own! And amazingly throughout the years whenever anyone has ever read it they thought it was meant for them! It was the only time I have felt "led" in that way---other than when I got involved in writing these stories (with an eighteen year hiatus between "inspirations")---but even now I vividly remember the awe with which I read the words that had poured forth after I sat at the typewriter in obedience.

During the time I thought I was just going to write down a few stories for my grandchildren (and before I ever believed they would become a *book!)* I looked high and low for a copy of "Butterflies," but I could not find one.

I called a few friends in different states to whom I recalled sending a copy many years earlier, and while all of them remembered it, none could find their copy either. I had just about exhausted my source of people who might be able to provide a copy for me and I didn't know where else to look. I went to my Tuesday morning women's Bible study and just as it was getting started I heard a woman several seats away whisper almost imperceptibly to the woman next to her, "I have the butterflies for you." My ears perked up. I said, "What did you say?" She replied, I just told my friend I had made a photocopy of something for her." I asked to see the paper and, lo and behold! it was my Butterflies story! It even had MY name on it! (The woman in the class knew my first name was Arlene, but she didn't know my last name). She said she had gotten it from her Compassionate Friends group, a support group for parents who have lost a child to cancer.

And so, through the mercy of God and the Compassionate Friends through whom He provided a copy of this inspired writing, here is "Butterflies":

Butterflies . . .

The butterfly is a fascinating creature. It is truly a work of art: beautiful colors and delicacy, flying high and wide on gossamer wings . . . free.

But the butterfly didn't begin its life in such a lofty state. In its earliest stages it was a caterpillar: crawly, slow, unattractive, plodding along, inch by inch. I wonder if ever in its wildest dreams it imagined what its destiny could be

Later in its development, it spent time locked in a cocoon of its own making---alone and perhaps even secure, warm and "safe." There, through the simple yielding of its nature to a Higher Nature, it became one of God's most wondrous and glorious creatures.

Before the transformation was complete, however, an intense and agonizing struggle had to be worked through. In order to become the magnificent creature it was destined to be, it first had a life-and-death struggle to work its way out of the cocoon---an exhausting and seemingly impossible task for such a delicate creature. Could it endure?

On one occasion, a well-meaning man watching this struggle decided to "help" the helpless butterfly, since it seemed such a gargantuan task for it to have to do on its own. So the man carefully sliced an opening in the cocoon with a razor blade and the butterfly was indeed able to get out much more easily. The problem was that the butterfly was never able to fly. You see, the struggle is actually part of the butterfly's way of BECOMING a butterfly, and the strength it gains *through the struggle* gives it the capability needed for flying. By "solving" the butterfly's problem, the man had created a flightless butterfly.

The butterfly's development from crawly, creeping caterpillar to glorious free-flying butterfly depends on the butterfly's acceptance and achievement of its *own* struggle-- on its faith that the struggle would lead it to something better.

If only man would accept his life and the changes in it with the same faith as that of the lowly caterpillar, perhaps he, too, would see that he could soar above his problems. We are called to prayer and trust and a willingness to wait in patient expectation. Will not our God who provides such a glorious end for the little caterpillar, provide for us in a way we cannot even envision?

(As a postscript, I see that this also pertains to how parents need to allow their children to face the natural consequences of their actions and how, at times, I am called to put my own little "razorblade" back into my pocket and allow the Lord to work without my help.)

Presents . . . Or Presence?

As I look back on the gifts I've received throughout my life, most of the time there is a link of "sentimental value" attached . . . a tangent not easily measured in monetary worth. Many times my most precious gifts have cost little when gauged by standards of financial value, but they touched my heart in an incalculable way.

During the time I worked for Birthright, 12-year old Scott came to me before Christmas and said, "Mom, I can't think of anything our family needs for Christmas this year, and I was thinking that the weather is getting cold now and those little babies might not have anything to keep them warm. I saw an ad for baby buntings, and I have saved enough money to buy six of them. Do you think our family would mind if I didn't use the money for them?" I wonder if he noticed the tender tear forming in the corner of my eye?

Another year, Christy told me about a family with six children whose father was out of work around Christmastime. She said they were too proud to accept "charity," but she knew they wouldn't have much of a Christmas. She asked if we could use some of the money we were going to spend on our family to buy items anonymously for each of the children, and then get some food from the Food Bank for them, too. We assembled everything she said we needed, wrapped gifts with notes to each recipient and put everything in two large boxes. We set off on our journey in the early hours of a Christmas morning. I parked the car about two houses away from their house so they would not hear the motor, then we crept up to the house in the dark and left the boxes on the porch. We ran back to the car so fast, with hearts beating wildly, that if we'd been seen by a policeman we looked so guilty we'd have had a hard time explaining that we were sneaking around *bringing* gifts, rather than stealing!

For Mother's Day one year, Billy gave me a lovely butterfly pin with wings that "fluttered," and I thought he'd spent too much money on me. He responded, "Look at it this way, Mom. It's only Monét!" And yes, it was only "Monét;" and if "Monét" isn't meant to be spent generously and joyously in giving, then what is it meant for? Years later when he was stationed in Korea, this same son had a waterproof jacket custom-made for me, with all the little zippered pockets and hood that I would need for hiking. (He had obviously remembered my tales of hiking in the woods and my need for waterproofing!) That same year Scott bought me a great pair of hiking shoes (also water-repellent) and spent more on them than I would have indulged on myself.

Billy once bought something he had to explain to me before I knew what it was. Many times I had asked the children to pull my boots off at the end of the day. The year that all of them were grown and gone, Billy bought me a wooden "bootjack" to help me get out of my boots, as evidence that he still thought of a way to be of service even in his absence.

And so, Lord, for the little remembrances You've brought to my recollection, I give you praise and thanksgiving and I ask forgiveness for those times I thought You did not know what You were doing by "blessing" me with three children in a four-year period. They are *indeed* blessings, and my understanding of the meaning of that is clearer with each passing year. It has nothing to do with what they *do*, but everything to do with who they *are* in Your Grand Plan.

"Would You Like a Candy Cane?"

Living on a farm has given me a graphic illustration of how important nourishment (food and water) is to all living things. Sometimes it's hard to get fertilizer and water to all the plants and trees that are in need. Times of dry spells cause distress, and on a 50-acre farm it is impossible to see that everything gets all it needs all the time. Our garden hoses have so many connections that we're now up to about 250' of pipeline. Nevertheless, the oscillating sprinkler regularly misses some of the vegetables and this lack is evident in the growth--not of the surrounding weeds, which thrive like well-fertilized/watered vegetation, but of my vegetable garden! I started thinking about this phenomenon. That which I *don't* want to grow, *thrives in neglect*; but the worthwhile vegetation takes much more focus and energy on my part.

Imagine the lonely, hurting, suffering people out there in our midst, whose lives need a touch of fertilizer or refreshing water to nourish their sagging spirits. I believe the Lord uses us as pieces of irrigation pipe to channel His loving care to those in need, and sometimes it takes lots of "connections" to provide the sustenance needed. Often we are just one small link in the process.

Each December for the past few years, I've bought about a hundred small candy canes and wrapped a small note around each one, tying it on with a piece of bright green yarn. Then I put about six to eight in my purse each day as I head out to do errands.

Whenever I encounter a harried or disgruntled person, in the post office or on a long line at a checkout counter or perhaps struggling with large packages in a parking lot, I say, "Would you like a candy cane?" I usually receive a surprised smile in return, and then wave good-by with, "Have a merry and peace-filled Christmas!" Unbeknownst to them, the little note wrapped around that candy cane just might give them pause in the hurried holiday season. Perhaps you've heard the story, but if not, here it is:

197

A Candy Maker's Witness

There once was a Candymaker who wanted to create a special confection to symbolize the birth, life and death of his Lord and Savior, so he started out with a pure, white base to symbolize the sinless and perfect nature of the Lord. It was hard candy to symbolize that the strength and faithfulness of the Lord is solid--like a Rock.

He formed it into the letter "J," to stand for Jesus. (When viewed upside down the shape also looks like a shepherd's staff, which the Divine Shepherd uses to gently guide and pull His errant flock back into the fold.) He put three narrow red stripes around it to stand for the scourging Jesus endured, and there was also a wider red stripe which represents the blood that Jesus shed to free mankind from the stain of sin.

Over the years it has become commonly known merely as a "Candy Cane," but the true meaning is still there for those with eyes to see and a heart to understand. I pray that you know the Savior and will experience the true peace and joy of this beautiful "holy-day" season, now and throughout all the days of your life.

Mission Possible: If you choose to accept the challenge, you can begin your own Candy Cane Caper in your own community. Think of the lives that could be touched by a sweet confection . . . and a smile from you.   If you'd like to use the story above in your own distribution, feel free to copy it and encourage others to do so, too. I think when we reach out to others---candy cane in hand---and add a smile to their day, we become what the Lord intends for us to be, a refreshing presence to others, in His name. Did you know we are called to be fertilizer for others? The Bible tells us so (only it uses the terms salt and light instead of "fertilizer.")

I believe there are lots of other ideas that would expand this mission effectively year-round as well. If any of you creative folks out there have felt led to other ways of touching people in the name of the Lord, drop me a note and let me know; my address is at the end of the book.

Raise Up a Child In the Way She Should Go . . .

I am a child of God and He is raising me in the way I should go. I **know** God answers prayer. He always answers prayer. Sometimes He says yes; sometimes He says no. And sometimes, like any conscientous parent, He says "wait." But He *always* answers. And like most petulant children, there are times I don't like His answer. Nevertheless, all children need wise and vigilant care.

I can remember occasions when one of my own children would burst in with a fast-talking request that required an answer from me. Often I would say, "If you need an immediate answer, it will be 'no,' but if you have time for me to think it over and weigh all the factors, it might be 'yes.' So if you are willing to wait, then the immediate answer for now is 'maybe'." They learned that "maybe" meant I was giving it serious consideration, and patience developed.

For everything there is a season. And what may be right and fitting in one season may not be so in another. Children have to depend on their parents and learn that they are trustworthy and reliable, even during those times when the answer is "no."

In the same way, my heavenly Father had many lessons that He wanted me to learn. First and foremost was "Love the Lord thy God with thy whole heart" and tacked onto that was "Seek ye FIRST the Kingdom of God and all these things will be added unto you." The way He led me was to have me lean fully on the truth of Psalm 119:105, "Thy word is a lamp unto my feet, and a light unto my path." And in times of trouble, doubt or fear, I have always found solace in His word. It illumines my way like no other "light" could.

Secondly, I discovered that I was to seek the Living Water to quench my soul; there is none other that can satisfy! After living on a farm, it is easy to see what an intregal and important role water has on anything that is growing. It is essential. And so is the refreshment found in the Lord vital to the human spirit! I have found this refreshment in His peace---the peace that transcends all human understanding. And that comes whenever I praise Him. In response to my praise, He *showers* down His peace on me!

Third, "Trust" was inextricably connected to my coming to know Him in a personal and intimate way. And linked arm-in-arm with Trust were the admonitions, "Fear not" and "Wait in patient expectation" and "Hope in the Lord." Little by little, these became part of my insight into His plan for me.

The Lord convicted me of the knowledge that I---along with all of mankind---am a sinner. It was then I began to understand the depth of His love and embrace His most incredible gift. No one can stand in the presence of a Holy God stained with a nature of sinfulness, and there is no way mere man can offer a suitable sacrifice in reparation. The reality of that truth makes His solution all the more awesome! Only a holy and spotless blood sacrifice could atone and make reparation to such a Holy God. In John 3:16, are the powerful words "For God so loved the world , that He gave His only begotten Son, that whosoever believes in Him should not perish, but have everlasting life." He provided His *own* blood sacrifice---His Son, Jesus---to restore me to full fellowship with Him. And though a narrow path, that bridge is wide enough for every person on this planet to walk across; it takes only sincere acknowledgment of one's need for a Savior, repentance for sinfulness, and acceptance of the Lord Jesus as the One through whom salvation is accomplished. Once we are washed in the Blood of the sacrificial Lamb, we are restored to a right relationship with God and are called to a life of trust and obedience. That doesn't mean I will never fall or err again, but when I do, the Holy Spirit will gently convict me and illumine the proper path. Note it doesn't say He will "condemn" me. Therein lies the difference in discerning whether the correction is from the Lord or the enemy. If from the Lord, I am persuaded and gently encouraged to change, but if from Satan, the father of lies, I merely feel "guilty" and hopeless.

I've always had my biggest difficulties with my tongue. I am not an "overt" sinner; that is to say, I do not wear my sins on my sleeve (i.e., I'm not an alcoholic, a murderer, an embezzler, etc.), but my sins are much more covert, and invariably come in the form of murder-by-tongue. Proverbs 18:21 spells out my affliction very graphically: "Death and life are in the power of the tongue." Whew!

A few years ago at a craft fair, I came upon a little plaque that seemed to have my name on it. It said: "Put Your Arm Around My Shoulder, Lord, and Your Hand Across My Mouth." I bought it. In fact, I bought two, one for the farmhouse where I'd see it six months of the year, and the other for the Ft. Lauderdale residence, so I wouldn't miss a single day's reminder of what my prayer needed to be. And I have to admit that ever since I've had those little visible reminders, my tongue has gotten noticably gentler. His admonition, "Be _still_ and know that I am God" has real meaning to me!

The Lord continues to confront me to see myself from His perspective, and to be willing to confess and turn from behavior that is unproductive and unfruitful. During a time of prayer and fasting, He brought renewed awareness to me of covert sinfulness--regarding attitudes in my life. The Lord showed me clearly that He views all sin in the same category as the blackest of sin. Such revelation and disclosure was a deeply moving experience---and an eye-opener! And while He love-love-_loves_ me unconditionally, He continues to fashion me into the person He created me to be.

It wasn't until after I had already initially written this chapter that I felt convicted that there was an important act of obedience missing on my part. Although I had been raised in a denomination that practiced infant baptism, I had never made a public profession of my desire to be baptized as an adult. So a few days before my 60th birthday, my pastor submerged this grandmother beneath the water, just as my Lord had subjected Himself when He was on earth. It was a humbling and incredible experience, and I had never before experienced both cold and hot water running down my face at the same time (from the pool water and my tears of gratitude).

The two churches the Lord has led me to in recent years are named "Calvary" in Ft. Lauderdale, and "House of Prayer" in Blairsville, and I know that both titles are meaningful in my life. When I think of Calvary--the site of my Lord's act of sacrifice for me--I am filled with wonder at the depth of love that God has for His people. And when I look at the stained glass window above the altar in Blairsville and see the words, "My House Shall Be Called a House of

Prayer for All People," it encourages my own prayer that *all* would come to a saving knowledge of this love.

Little by little, my Father is growing me up. And I know that raising this child in the way I should go, means that when I am old (or old-*er*), I will not depart from it. And that is one of the most important lessons He is teaching me: Perseverance. It is not running the race that is important; it is finishing it---and finishing well. Thousands of people start running a marathon each year; and each one of them stops running at some point. But not all *finish the race*. As for me, I want to claim the prize at the finish line, where my Father waits for me, cheering me on. My desire is to be "cloaked in a garment of thanksgiving" and found faithful to the end.

Postscript: After this book had been sent off to production and was in the midst of being proofed at the publisher's, I was impacted by a final word that just seemed to need to be added to this book. I spent four days at the home of a friend whom I hadn't seen in many years. She and her husband hosted me while I did a quilt show in their city. Their home provided an aura of peace and calm in the midst of a long, grueling schedule, and they saw to it that our dinner times and evenings were filled with relaxation and laughter. But what really impacted me most about my visit was a small name card she had placed in my bedroom. (*I've always wondered what would happen if someone shouted, "Stop the presses!" and now I know.*) The card said:

> **Arlene**............"*Faithful*"
> And the Lord, *He* it is that doth
> go before thee; He will not fail
> thee, neither forsake thee: fear
> not, neither be dismayed.
> Deuteronomy 31:8

Each morning during my stay, when I awoke I would hold that little card in my hand and meditate on the depth of meaning within those few words and how I had found them to be true throughout my life. And my fervent prayer is that each person who reads this book will come to an awareness that it was true in his or her life as well.

Notes

Although I never set out to "write a book," somehow by the grace of God, it got written. And despite my lack of marketing skills, somehow the first printing got sold out in record time. It would be hard to fail to recognize His hand and not give God the glory for that!

It never fails to bless my heart to hear from people throughout the country who have received the book as a gift and who want to order additional copies to pass along to friends. Each time someone shares how the book has impacted them, I know they have been touched by the hand of God, and it is humbling to imagine that He has used such an "Ordinary Person" like me to reach out to His people. But then I think back to *all* the ordinary people He used throughout history . . . including David, whose father didn't even think to include him when told to assemble all his sons--for he was "just a boy." Nevertheless, where others saw merely a shepherd boy, God saw a king. (And when He sees me, He sees a princess, daughter of *The* King!)

If after reading this book you'd like to share any thoughts, you can drop me a note at the following address:

> Arlene M.Gray
> God's Country Farm
> 2222 Country Farm Lane
> Blairsville, GA 30512

Additional copies of this book may also be ordered directly by sending a check or money order payable to Arlene M. Gray as follows:

> 1-4 copies $8.95 each, plus $1.75 S&H for *first* copy (Book Rate) or $3.00 (Priority Mail), and $1.00 for *each additional copy*
>
> 5 or more copies $7.95 each, plus $1.00 S&H for each copy. Georgia residents, please add 6% sales tax.

(over)

Please print your name and address clearly and send it, along with payment for the number of books ordered, to the address above, and if you would like your books autographed, kindly print the name of the recipient(s) if personalization is requested.

. . . .

I'd also like to recommend another book I know you'd enjoy:

ANGEL FEATHERS by Tammy M. Floyd, is a wonderful collection of extraordinary stories that remind us that no matter what our circumstances, God takes notice---and sometimes miraculously intervenes in our everyday lives to show us how much He loves us. On occasion His performances are as dramatic as lightning bolts; other times He comes to us in the "still, small voice." Tammy has compiled over forty true stories of divine intervention, delightfully presented to touch your heartstrings.

Send check or money order for $8.95 plus $1.75 S&H, to Tammy M. Floyd, 4126 S. Mauney Road, Blairsville, GA 30512. *You'll be glad you did!*